Worth the Wait

Tales of the 2008 Phillies

Jayson Stark

TRIUMPH
BOOKS

Triumph Books and colophon are registered trademarks of Random House, Inc.

Library of Congress Cataloging-in-Publication Data

Stark, Jayson, 1951–
  Worth the wait : tales of the 2008 Phillies / by Jayson
Stark.
     p. cm.
  ISBN 978-1-60078-273-2
  1. Philadelphia Phillies (Baseball team) I. Title.
  GV875.P45S735 2009
  796.357'640974811—dc22

                                              2009002358

This book is available in quantity at special discounts for your group or organization. For further information, contact:
   Triumph Books
   542 South Dearborn Street
   Suite 750
   Chicago, Illinois 60605
   (312) 939-3330
   Fax (312) 663-3557

Printed in U.S.A.
ISBN: 978-1-60078-273-2
Design by Patricia Frey
Photos courtesy of AP Images unless otherwise indicated

To one of the truly special people on this planet, the vivacious love of my life, Lisa Stark, whose love completes me, whose friendship lifts me, and whose incredible heart has inspired me from the moment I met her

Contents

Acknowledgments

Let's roll back the clock to February 6, 2005. That was the day the three beautiful children in the Stark household—Steven, Jessica, and Hali—gathered with their mom and dad around the television for a day they figured was going to be unlike any in their lifetimes.

And by that I mean the day they finally saw one frigging team from their good old hometown, Philadelphia, win something. Anything.

In this case, that something was supposed to be the Super Bowl. So they sat there for the next four hours and watched those heartless New England Patriots crush their still-innocent young dreams, not to mention the Eagles. And when it was over, the Stark children knew there was only one way to handle the pain: Leave town. Forever.

"Dad?" Hali said, finally. "Can we move?"

She meant it, too. I think. She'd lived her whole life in Philadelphia, and she'd never once experienced that legendary thrill-of-victory euphoria she'd heard so much about. So this was the most practical solution out there, she figured: Move. Adopt somebody else's town. Why the heck not? No good was coming from living in *her* town.

I never forgot that day. And it wasn't because I was crushed by that loss. Why would I be? I'm not a fan the way my wife and kids are fans. I don't get emotionally consumed by sports; I cover sports for a living. But to see that look in my kids' eyes, to see the hope vacuumed out of them, to hear the sheer misery in their voices, now that was tough.

No day in my whole existence sledgehammered home the true real-life significance of sports in the lives of your average humans the way that day did. So this book, first of all, is for the Stark kids. They saw their baseball team win a World Series with their very own eyes. And they didn't even have to move.

So thanks to my kids for teaching me such an indelible lesson about the powerful meaning of it all.

And thanks to my awesome wife, Lisa, who thought from the beginning that the 2008 Phillies were a runaway best-selling book waiting to happen. I recognize exactly how lucky I am to have a wife who is such a never-ending source of inspiration, driving me to accomplish bigger and better things every day, every month, every year.

Thanks, too, to ESPN, for literally making this possible. For originally publishing many of these words in the first place. And for giving me permission to publish them again here. I owe a special debt of gratitude to Steve Wulf and Glen Waggoner, of ESPN's publishing division, for paving the way for this book to happen. I'd also like to direct a major *gracias* to ESPN research guru Mark Simon for making certain I'd always have an unlimited supply of invaluably useless October information. And I don't even know how to begin properly thanking my amazing baseball editors at ESPN.com—Dave Kull, Marty Bernoski, Matt Szefc, and Nick Pietruszkiewicz. No single living American has cost all of them more sleep in the month of October than I have. But they've never hesitated to give me all the time and space I thought I needed to tell the stories of these games the way they deserve to be told.

To my relentlessly upbeat editors at Triumph Books—Tom Bast, Don Gulbrandsen, and Laine Morreau—I say thanks for having the vision to see that this was a project worth pursuing, and for rearranging your schedules to make it happen so quickly.

And, finally, I'd like to raise a champagne glass to salute one of the least-appreciated segments of the entire human race—the remarkable sports fans who live all around me in the great metropolis of Philadelphia. Never in the history of mankind have 5 million people needed the joy a sports team gave them more than these people needed that World Series. You can only eat heartbreak for breakfast, lunch, and dinner for so many years, you know, before it starts to drain something out of you. Something important. Something special. Yeah, it's only sports, so it shouldn't matter. They know that. We all know that. But all those years of disappointment were beginning to affect the way too many of my favorite people felt about, well, everything—their own town and their own teams and even their own lives. Then something happened in their friendly neighborhood ballpark that changed all that. I've seen it. I've felt it. As a guy who has lived in Philly nearly all my life, I get it.

As I walked around South Philly on the day of the World Series parade, I was blown away by how many people stopped to thank me for the way I told their baseball team's story. And to tell me how much it meant to them that I understood *them*—and what their team's astonishing October journey did for their friends, their family, and their city. If so many of those people hadn't expressed those thoughts, this book never would have happened. Philadelphians kept telling me, over and over, "You should put all your Phillies columns in a book. I'd buy it." Well, thanks for the suggestion. But we did even better than that. We took those columns, reshaped them, and added thousands of words of new material. And the result is a book that takes you on a voyage with the 2008 Phillies, from the opening days of spring training to the day the parade floats blitzed through town. I don't think you have to be a Philadelphian to enjoy the ride, but if you are a Philadelphian, you should know this book was written for you. But more than that, it was also inspired by you. So thanks to every one of you for giving me the motivation to put this project into words. I hope it was worth the wait.

Introduction

Free at Last

The clock had ticked to the edge of midnight on the Night the Phillies Won the World Series. The clubhouse of the champs had finally grown quiet. The champagne-soaked plastic sheets had been ripped off the lockers, and the emptied bottles of Domaine Ste. Michelle had been tossed into America's most overloaded recycling bins.

And Jimmy Rollins, the visionary who had once imagined this scene in his brain long before the rest of civilization, was getting ready to burst out into the night, the craziest Philadelphia night of his lifetime. Except before he could slip out the locker-room door, he ran headlong into...me.

I'd known him longer than just about any player in that room. I'd known him since he first showed up in Philadelphia—all 5'8", 165 pounds of him—in September 2000, at age 21, for the final weeks of another lost journey to the bottom of the standings. We'd shared a thousand conversations and a thousand baseball moments over those last eight years, but we'd never shared this. The Phillies—his Phillies—were heading for the parade floats. And Jimmy Rollins, a man never at a loss for words, was still trying to grasp the life-changing immensity of what had just happened.

"I can't even understand it right now," he said. "I can't do it."

So I tried to help. We began to talk about what was already happening beyond those ballpark walls, in this town he played baseball in, in this town I'd lived in most of my life. For years, for decades, these people had been so consumed by the accumulation of all this frustration that kept swallowing them whole, it was almost as if they woke up every morning and thought, *Who can I boo today?* And now, already, they were different: transformed, liberated. After a quarter-century of waiting for a team like this to end their torment, that team had finally arrived. This team. Jimmy Rollins' team.

"You realize," I told him, "you've set all these people free."

He laughed.

"Prison break, huh?" he quipped.

Right; prison break. After 25 years of heartbreak, 25 years of never-ending misery inflicted by four star-crossed teams in four professional sports, these people had finally tunneled their way out of their excruciating sports torture chamber. This was their first chance to bask in a title—*any* kind of title, in *any* of those sports—since Moses Malone's 1982–83 76ers, a team that existed 25 years and more than 9,000 games deep in their rearview mirror. And leading the way to that title was—how did this happen?—the local baseball team. The losingest team in North American sports history. The team whose claim to fame was dragging about 87 generations of Philadelphians through one agonizing season after another. This, for years, had been the team these people had the least faith in. So how amazing was it that this was the team that had finally set them free?

"For all those years," said Mike Missanelli, dulcet voice of Philadelphia's ESPN 950 radio airwaves, "your grandfather looked at this team and said, 'These bums will never win.' And your father said, 'These bums will never win.' And *you* said, 'These bums will never win.' And then, all of a sudden, they won. How often has that happened to these people?"

People line Broad Street in Philadelphia on October 31, 2008, to wave to players during a parade celebrating the Phillies' World Series victory over the Tampa Bay Rays.

To some of them? How about never. Ever. This was a life experience with which many of these folks had zero familiarity whatsoever. They knew as much about the migration patterns of wild caribou as they knew about how to act when a team in their very own town actually won something.

"When they won, I didn't know what to do," said one resident of that strange new world, 28-year-old Brian Turcich. "I was in a bar with about 20 friends. The place was packed. And when they got the final out, there was like a pause, like, *Did that just happen?* Then everyone started hugging and kissing and high-fiving all the way down the street. But it was just such a weird situation. No one really knew what to do, because you've got this whole generation of kids who had never won a championship."

So as you try to contemplate that tidal wave of emotions that engulfed him and all those people like him at that metamorphic moment, there is something important you need to understand before this book marches onward for even one more paragraph: When something like this happens, this is *not* a sports story. This is a life story.

A sports story is when somebody wins and somebody loses; you spend 75 bucks on tickets, parking, and cheesesteaks; and then you go home and resume your regularly scheduled life.

A life story is when something happens on a baseball field and tears start overflowing your face. And you find yourself calling everyone you've ever cared about in your entire life and telling them this is the happiest moment in the history of the solar system, even better than that day you met Tina Fey in the airport. And then you listen to everyone in all of your households shriek and sob and laugh and pop champagne corks right there in the kitchen. And then you're blowing off work, you're yanking your kids out of school, you're navigating the traffic jam from hell, and you're abandoning your car in a tow-away zone in center city, all because nothing in your regular life matters more than joining 2 million euphoric humans—2 million people who, by some inexplicable miracle, suddenly feel exactly like you do—for a parade that makes the Tournament of Roses look like a little skit down at your kids' preschool.

And you know what? The more I reflect on it, the more I realize that that word *parade* doesn't even come close to describing what took place in the city of Philadelphia on the final day of October 2008. Oh, there were floats and confetti and all those customary parade accoutrements. But this was way too big, way too powerful as a life experience, to be described as a mere parade.

"I don't think I've ever seen a parade like that," said the man who somehow became the ultimate grand parade master that day, manager Charlie Manuel. "I don't think there's ever *been* a parade like that. That's the greatest thing I've ever seen in my whole life. When we won, I knew it would be a big deal. But I had no idea it would be *that* big, that we made that many people happy, that we made that many people celebrate something."

What the manager saw that day, what all these men saw that day, was a sight they didn't know was possible. They saw people whose whole lives had changed. And I'm not exaggerating when I say that, either. That really happened. These people had just had their entire image of themselves, their community, and pretty much every single human being around them completely rearranged. Seriously.

Yeah, yeah, I know that to people on the outside, this might have seemed like the same old basic plotline you see every single frigging year: Team wins, fans happy. But on the inside, these people knew this was more than that, huger than that. I don't know to explain how something that happens in a mere sporting event could be that meaningful to that many people, way, way, wayyyyy down there in the cores of their souls.

But it was. It happened. I was there, hanging out with my euphoric daughter Hali, so I saw it. And the baseball players who made it happen saw it. And they, too, may never look at fans—*any* fans—the same way because of what they saw.

"I'll be honest. I can't imagine having that kind of impact on a city, on the people in a city," said third baseman and pinch-hit king Greg Dobbs. "It really blows your mind. You know, for the most part, we're in kind of our own little bubble as athletes. But...I saw grown men and women crying as we were passing by. Literally crying. You know, I'm just a baseball player. That's what I do. I don't hold myself up on any pedestal; I play baseball. And then here I am on this float...with people looking me in the eye and thanking me, with tears flowing down their faces, for bringing them a championship. That's beyond anything I ever imagined. I get goose bumps just thinking about it. That's an experience that's going to live with me for the rest of my life."

The tears. The men who rode on those floats keep talking about the tears. And the faces. The looks on the faces. You don't see those looks often in life, especially not on 2 million of those faces at once. Theoretically, that ought to be impossible, right? To have that many people walking around at the same time on the same day, wearing that same look in their eyes—that blissful, life-is-great glow you wait your whole life for?

"That's the thing that really got to me, that became my No. 1 moment in baseball," said Phillies chairman Bill Giles, a man who rode down the same parade route with the only other World Series championship team in Phillies history, back in 1980. "To see the real love in the faces of all those people was unbelievable. It wasn't quite that way in '80. Just the expressions of admiration and love on the faces of those people was awesome.

"I wouldn't have used that word *love* in 1980," Giles went on. "It was more a 'thank you.'... But this was different. And it was because of these

Xanadu. And that just kind of breeds this inferiority complex in the whole town. But that changed when this thing rolled through town."

This, ladies and gentlemen, is the power of sports. It makes no sense that something as theoretically unimportant as sports could be the best psychotherapy ever invented. But you'll never convince the lucky residents of the Philadelphia metropolitan area that it's not. Not now. Not when the buzz of winning is still fresh enough that they almost don't care that their stock portfolios have plummeted to approximately the same worth as the contents of their refrigerators' produce bins.

Life, for these people, is good. The only question is: How good? And the only question after that is: How long can this buzz possibly last? And the honest answer is: Way, way, way longer than you'd ever think.

It's nearly three decades now since Dallas Green managed the first Phillies team to win a World Series. And all these years later, when I asked him what it's been like to walk around Philadelphia, knowing how people still revere that feat, his voice actually quivered before he answered, "I don't have the ability to describe it.

"The pride I have in wearing this [World Series] ring and being recognized as the only guy who had it for 28 years has just been wonderful for me and my family," he said. "I've just never gotten over it to this day.... Let's face it, it springboarded my whole career."

Of course, that title hung there, all alone, in the Philadelphia sky for so long that no wonder the men responsible for it remain such indelible icons. Who was supposed to join them in that pantheon—Ricky Otero? Jerry Spradlin? Steve Jeltz? The only parade those guys rode in was their parade right out of town.

So obviously, we don't know how long Philadelphians are going to have to wait for That Next Parade. But here's a bet: It won't change the way they feel about the team that gave them *this* parade.

"All my buddies told me, back in 1980, that I'd never have to buy another beer in Philadelphia," Green said. "And they're probably right. These people don't forget. And I really appreciate the fact that they don't forget."

So for Charlie Manuel, this love affair looks as if it just might be for life. For Shane Victorino, Brad Lidge, Jimmy Rollins, and all the architects of this little prison break, it would take some serious screwing up to make their adoring public forget the way those men made their city feel in the magical month of October 2008.

We know and they know the months ahead won't all feel that good. We know and they know the seasons ahead won't all end on parade floats. We know and they know that this is still Philadelphia, so sooner or later, there will be sounds flowing down from those seats that won't remind them of the sounds they heard The Night The Phillies Won the World Series.

But that could be the ultimate test of the magnitude of winning. Is it actually possible that in Philadelphia, of all places, even the booing might not be the same?

"Oh, yeah. They'll still boo," said Phillies broadcast witticist Larry Andersen. "They *have* to. They're born to boo.

"Just now," Larry Andersen chuckled, "they'll only boo with two Os instead of like four."

Part 1

Dawn of a Championship Season

I've been listening to teams tell their spring-training stories for about three decades now. So I know the deal. Let these teams bake in the spring sunshine when they haven't lost a game in four months, and everybody talks like they've fixed everything but the trade deficit. Spring training is a time for dreaming. I know that. But when the 2008 Phillies showed up beneath the Clearwater palms, there was something different about them. When this team talked, it wasn't just the same old spring-training yapping. Winning the NL East in 2007 had changed these men, transported them to a different place, a place you can't get to on United Airlines. They now knew what winning tasted like, smelled like, sounded like. And it provided them with a sense of purpose that drove them all the way to the parade floats eight months later. I wrote this piece on February 29. Looking back on it now, I've never felt more Nostradamus-like.

Playing Those Mind Games Forever

CLEARWATER, FLORIDA—You don't only measure winning in the standings; you also measure it in the mind.

So this is a tale about what happens in that mind—in 25 minds, to be exact—when a team wins that hasn't won. A team that has been told, in fact, that it can't win, won't win, doesn't know how to win.

And then, amazingly, that same team wins in a way that should be just about impossible, in a way that makes history. In a way that changes everyone involved—but not on the outside. On the inside, in that orb above the eyebrows where the brainwaves reverberate.

This is a tale about the spring-training mind-set of the 2008 Phillies, a baseball team full of people whose brainwaves couldn't ever be the same again. Not after making up seven games with 17 to play in September 2007 to steal the National League East from the Mets.

"There's a feeling," said Jimmy Rollins, the MVP/psychology major of this group. "But the feeling can't really be expressed in words. It's just, you *know*. You know you're in a group that's going to win. You know what everybody's focus is. It's on winning."

Other years, with other Phillies teams, it wasn't like that. You might have noticed that. Other years, the focus was on other stuff, stuff that didn't involve a single champagne cork. Stuff like, well, *survival.*

Most teams go to spring training dreaming those October dreams. The Phillies of the late '90s and early '00s went to spring training dreaming of just avoiding disaster. The magic word wasn't *winning* then. The most optimistic word ever thrown at them was (ahem) *competitive.*

"That was kind of like the theme—be competitive," Rollins reminisced, not very nostalgically. "Even in our spring-training meetings, it was like, 'Let's go out there and be competitive.' But it was really like, 'We *want* to be more than competitive—*but.*'

"Even though they didn't say, 'but,' you always knew there was a 'but': 'But we're going to be undermanned,' or, 'But we're not going to have the talent,' or 'We just don't quite know how to get there yet, but we'll learn; everybody's young.' But after a while, you're not going to be young too much longer."

Yes, after a while, the years seemed to be whooshing by for this group, until these guys *weren't* young anymore. The years began to take on a familiar pattern—the traditional gruesome start, followed by the just-as-traditional tantalizing near-miss.

That was their story, year after year. Two games behind the Braves in 2001; a half-game wild-card lead disappearing in the final week in 2003; one win too few in the 2005 wild-card race; three wins too few in the 2006 wild-card race.

Was this a team growing slowly toward success? Or was this a bunch of players who were trapped inside their own reputation as a team that could never quite find the last trail up the mountain?

"When I first got here," said manager Charlie Manuel, who first joined this organization as a special advisor in 2003, "I felt like [that winning attitude] wasn't there. I felt like we had some real good players,

Jimmy Rollins takes infield practice at baseball spring training in February 2008.

but putting up numbers or making the All-Star team might have come before anything else. Not that we weren't thinking about winning. But I felt like just playing and [advancing] their careers came first."

Back then, though, Manuel wasn't the manager either. A fellow named Larry Bowa was. Bowa breathed the fire of winning, but while he raised the bar for everyone around him, he was also more a master of intimidation than inspiration.

So when Bowa was gonged after 2004 and the easygoing Manuel took the reins, the team he inherited couldn't possibly have been more grateful for a different approach.

"I was always cool with Bo, but Charlie came in with a different atmosphere, which made it easier," Rollins said. "It took the militant ways out. You know what I'm saying? And it was like, 'Baseball's a game. Let's go have fun.'

"And when you have fun, you remember how to win, because you're not worried about making the mistake. You're not worried about doing something wrong.... You can come to the park the next day, and you know the manager is still going to talk to you. And the coaching staff is still going to talk to you.

"Before, it was like, 'If you didn't get four hits, I don't want to talk to you today. Don't say hi to me if I don't say hi to you.' That's just the way it was. And those aren't winning ways.... It was more about conduct than it was about winning."

But while the approach changed and the clubhouse relaxed, one thing stayed constant: Manuel's seasons didn't end much different from Bowa's. Until 2007. And 2007 changed everything and everybody.

"We've jumped that curb now," said Brett Myers, about to launch his seventh season as a Phillie. "That was just a hurdle that we had to achieve. And now, it's a lot easier to know what it takes. I mean, a lot of us really hadn't tasted that.

"I had always known it takes hard work and dedication," Myers said. "But what it really takes is a *team*."

We know there are still people on this planet who believe chemistry in baseball is a hoax, a myth, a slice of fiction perpetrated by media knuckleheads who don't know any better. But we wish those people luck trying to convince *this* group of that.

Not so long ago, as Charlie Manuel said, the men who wore the Phillies uniform were preoccupied with their own numbers, their own paychecks, their own rationales for never quite getting it right.

Now, said Rollins, these guys are "more focused on *we* need to get right. Not *you* get right, and *you* get right, and *you* get right. *We're* going to get right. We're going to *be* right.... Now it doesn't matter who gets it done. We don't care about who the hero is."

Back when Bobby Abreu was the Phillies' centerpiece player, Rollins can recall being sent to the plate to "get on base for Bobby." Now that *he's* a centerpiece player, hitting in front of bats like Chase Utley and Ryan Howard, he heads for the plate in the same kinds of situations, with the mindset that *somebody* will make it happen.

"Before," Rollins said, "it was like, 'Let's try to get Bobby up there and we'll have a chance.' Now I have confidence that if I don't get it done, somebody will get it done behind me. Now we have a *team*."

Now they also have real leaders, in Rollins and Utley, who took over the clubhouse—and the chemistry lab—once Abreu was exported to the Bronx in July 2006.

"To me, [they're] the two out-and-out leaders on this team," said Jamie Moyer, a man getting ready for his 22nd season of observing big-league clubhouses. "Not just on the field. In how they play the game and approach the game. In their work ethic, on the field, off the field. How they act toward people, treat people, talk to people, act toward their teammates."

The Last Trail up the Mountain

After he first signed with the Phillies out of high school, Jimmy Rollins says, he was almost embarrassed to tell people back home in Oakland he was a Phillie. It "wasn't cool," he says, to play for a team that never, ever, seemed to show up in October, that never, ever, reminded the population of America it was still in business.

"We had nothing to really reflect on," he says. "In 1980 [when they won the World Series], I was two. In '93 [last time they played in a World Series], I was a freshman, sophomore in high school. So we really had nothing to pull from as far as being successful as an organization. So you had no pride."

Prior to their 2007 wild-card berth, the Phillies hadn't played a postseason game in 14 years. They were a team that began to specialize in gruesome starts, followed by tantalizing near-misses: Two games behind the Braves in 2001, a half-game wild-card lead disappearing in the final week in 2003, one win too few in the 2005 wild-card race, and three wins too few in the 2006 wild-card race.

Looking back on those years now, they all helped lead this group to this place and this time. But back then, they didn't feel that way. Back then, they just fueled the reputation of a team that could never quite find the last trail up the mountain.

"[We] were learning, just taking those baby steps toward having success," Rollins says now. "But it was still like, 'Well, they're just going to be good enough to come in second to the Atlanta Braves.' It was like, 'Don't worry about the playoffs. Just be competitive.' And that was kind of like the theme, even in spring-training meetings."

You know those famous predictions by Jimmy Rollins in the 2007 and 2008 off-seasons? They weren't about the shortstop trying to irritate the Mets or trying to be Nostradamus. They were about leadership.

"I'm not just running my mouth just to be noticed," Rollins said. "I do this for a reason. I talk for a reason. I'm trying to help people for a reason. I'm enlisting you to help *me* for a reason. It's not all about me. It's not all about *I*. It's about one goal—changing this organization to a winning organization."

Rollins and Utley approach that leadership with "no ego," Moyer said. "So nobody has that 'I-don't-have-to-take-BP-today' attitude, or 'I don't have to run.' Everybody is accountable. And if somebody gets side-tracked, it seems to get taken care of."

So a lot of what was different here had been evolving for two years, at times imperceptibly. But what happened in the final weeks of 2007, as this team thundered from behind, propelled these men past their final psychological barrier in one volcanic eruption.

"I see a more confident group of guys this spring," Manuel said on a cloudless February afternoon. "The expectations of these guys are huge. We definitely expect to win. It's not even a question. We're gonna win."

"You're no longer questioning yourself," Rollins said. "You no longer feel like you have to answer to questions that aren't being asked, but they're getting written about. People give you a break. I'll give you an example: I haven't heard one speech this year about 'We have to get off to a good start.' Why? Because we finally won something."

For the last decade, though, that isn't how it's been. For years, *We Have to Get Off to a Good Start* was practically stamped on every forehead in this clubhouse. Not without reason, you understand, for a franchise that had had two winning Aprils in the last 11 seasons.

So one stinking loss on Opening Day *always* seemed to unleash all the negative energy that's forever lurking in that city they play in. And that one stinking loss *always* seemed to mushroom into a 1–6 start and a 9–14 April.

"Now," said Rollins, "we're past getting off to a good start. We're thinking, *Win, win, win, win, win.* It's, *Let's go out and win the division.*

Let's go out and try to be a world-championship team. Those are the things that are in our head now."

They knew how good the Mets were. They knew how good the Braves were. They talked respectfully about the Nationals and Marlins. But the clear difference between these Phillies and the teams that came before them was this: They knew how good *they* were.

"What have we learned? It's the urgency of knowing how to win, knowing how to play like you need this game today," Rollins said. "You learn those things. In the past, we coasted through those things. It was like, 'Damn, we didn't get off to another good start. Here we go again.' Now it's not about the game we lost. It's about the next game."

What's next was a big topic in the clubhouse—in more ways than one. Much as they enjoyed winning what they won, these men also talked openly about what they still *hadn't* won.

"I don't want to downplay it," said Moyer, "but we didn't win the World Series, either.... We're not here to go through the motions and live off last year."

That focus on What's Next was why you didn't hear the shortstop talking anymore about who the team to beat was. Jimmy Rollins raised that bar again—to 100 wins.

"We won last year, and I want to win this year," Rollins said. "But I don't want it to come down to the last day of the season...89 wins barely got us in. It showed how good a team we ended up being. But it didn't show from the start how good we were."

"Now we should know from the start how good we are," said this team's professor of psychology. "Don't guess, '*Can* you win?' You know that answer now."

Oh, there was definitely reason to debate whether this team had enough pitching to win 100 games—or even beat out the Mets and

Braves. And there was cause to dissect whether this team made enough contact or had enough prospects to sustain what it's built.

But this wasn't a tale about those kinds of *X*s and *O*s. This was a tale about the Battle of the Brain.

And this was one Phillies team that finally seemed to have that battlefield all mapped out.

It's a funny thing about the Phillies and the Mets. For four stinking decades, they couldn't put a decent rivalry together with a Lego set. When the Mets were good, the Phillies stunk. When the Phillies were good, the Mets stunk. So it doesn't matter how one city feels about another city. It doesn't matter how fast one team's fans can commute to the other team's ballpark. It doesn't matter that you could keep a panel of psychologists busy round the clock with Philadelphians trying to deny they have a New York inferiority complex. It doesn't matter because, to be a real rivalry, you need two teams that are good enough to make all the rest of that stuff matter. Well, the Mets and Phillies finally made it to that place. And once they achieved official rival-hood, it's safe to announce they definitely got the hang of it.

This was a column I wrote on February 17, 2008—a day that rivalry escalated to a whole new stratosphere. An Ali-Frazier kind of stratosphere. A Duke-Carolina kind of stratosphere. A T.O.-Donovan kind of stratosphere. And we could tell because the Mets' Carlos Beltran had just arrived in spring training. And he apparently arrived with Jimmy Rollins' 2007 quote of the year still stuck in his abdomen and his memory bank. So he came out with a quote of his own. And this was the day the Phillies answered back. Vince McMahon couldn't have scripted this one better himself.

Oh, and one other thing. This isn't the only chapter in this book that contains material first published on ESPN.com. The preceding chapter and most of the accounts of the 2008 postseason also fit that description. But unlike almost all that other material, which was reworked and adapted for this book, I've left this piece virtually unchanged from the version I wrote the day it all exploded. It captured a slice of NL East life that is still best summed up by allowing it to stay frozen in that moment. So consider this a little five-page trip in the time capsule, back to the craziest day of spring training 2008.

The Rivalry Erupts

January 23, 2007, from Phillies shortstop Jimmy Rollins:
"I think we *are* the team to beat—finally."

February 16, 2008, from Mets center fielder Carlos Beltran:
"This year, tell Jimmy Rollins *we're* the team to beat."

CLEARWATER, FLORIDA—For those of us who cover spring training for a living, there's only one thing better than a little mid-February trash-talking. And no, it's *not* being told that our tans look marvelous. No, sirree. Here's the one thing that—oops, hold on a second while we wipe that sunscreen out of our eyes—is way better than trash-talk: The rivalries that *inspire* the trash-talk.

Well, we've got one, friends. We've got ourselves a good one. There we all were, minding our business, agonizing over that critical choice between SPF 15 or 30, when one of the best rivalries in baseball officially erupted before our sun-drenched eyeballs: Phillies-Mets.

Who knew? All it took was Carlos Beltran announcing in Port St. Lucie that *his* team was the team to beat. And presto—Phillies-Mets had instantly zoomed right to the top of the National League rivalry charts.

We acknowledge that Dodgers-Giants and Cubs-Cardinals have more history. So hold those emails. But this is about 2008, not 1951. And in 2008, we challenge you to find two teams in the NL that are more closely matched—and more obsessed with each other—than these two.

Oh, the Mets have long been on the Phillies' radar screens. That's nothing new. But now it's the year after Jimmy Rollins' stunning team-to-beat prediction came true. The year after an epic Mets September collapse and a rousing Phillies charge to the finish line.

So when a guy like Beltran—who normally doesn't raise his voice much above a murmur—is sending carefully calculated messages to the Phillies through the media, that's a sign we're now in a different realm. We're now in a realm where the Phillies have actually infiltrated the Mets' radar screen, too. And that tells us we're in for a fun summer in the old NL East.

"It's amazing how fast this has become such a great rivalry," said Phillies center fielder Shane Victorino. "First, Jimmy makes his statement. Now Carlos is making his statement. It's becoming like, 'Who's going to say something next?'"

"Well," we observed, "if you'd like to volunteer...."

"Noooooo," Victorino laughed. "No comments out of this guy."

But fortunately for you trash-talk fans, we didn't quit there. Across the room, we found Phillies pitcher Brett Myers, a man who wasn't quite so reticent to wander into this fray.

Myers, it turned out, was well aware of Beltran's comments—possibly because he'd been asked approximately 9,758 questions about them already. And it wasn't even lunchtime yet.

"If that's his way of learning from the MVP how to fire up his team, that's fine," Myers quipped, eyes twinkling. "I hope it works for him—just not against us."

As a guy who once aspired to be a boxer growing up, Myers never met a battle he thought was worth backing away from. So he dropped a reference to Rollins' most famous pronouncement from *this* winter—that the Phillies were going to win 100 games. Then Brett Myers essentially accused Beltran of a truly heinous crime—trash-talk plagiarism.

"Sequels are terrible," Myers deadpanned. "You can't predict it twice. That's why Jimmy went with his sequel of 100 wins. The plot has changed for us. I guess their favorite movie was us last year, or something. I don't know.

"But if they're trying to shake us up, they're not going to, because we're too strong-minded and strong-willed."

What they want to do, of course, is exactly what the Mets want to do (and the Braves, too, by the way—but they keep forgetting to trash-talk about it). These are teams dreaming very big dreams; dreams that involve champagne, ticker tape, and a tee-time–free October; dreams that, hopefully, will not be narrated by Dane Cook.

But to achieve those dreams, the Phillies and Mets need to vanquish the team on the other end of that rivalry. So let the war of words begin—all in good fun, of course.

"You know what? *We're* the team to beat," said Phillies reliever Tom Gordon. "That's what I think. I think we're good. This is a tough team. So don't say I'm coming back with talk, because that's not what I'm doing. All I'm saying is, I believe that we're a good team that can win a championship."

But to win a championship, a team needs to be tested. And that's where those rivalries come in. Tom Gordon should know. He has pitched for the Red Sox. He has pitched for the Yankees. He has pitched in the glow of the fieriest rivalry in baseball.

So while he understands that the Phillies and Mets aren't quite in that league, they now have a chance to live out something special.

"I played with the Royals first," Gordon said. "When I played with the Royals, I don't remember a rivalry. I remember us going to play and trying to win every game we could win. But I don't remember games like that, where you'd come to the stadium and there's people everywhere, screaming and excited about their team.

"I'd never seen anything like it till I got to Boston and New York. And now I see it with Philadelphia and the Mets. It's great for the game. Nothing wrong with a little trash-talking. It's all in good humor. Guys have fun with it."

Now, perhaps you worry that not everyone will understand the nature of all that fun. Perhaps you worry that somewhere along the line, if this talk keeps up, this rivalry could turn messy. Ugly even.

Well, fortunately, these two teams play in mellow, laid-back markets where fans believe in showering their opponents with respect and admiration. Where the folks in the seats can be counted on to take this stuff in the light-hearted spirit in which it's all intended. Okay, so maybe not.

So we probably have to allow for the slight possibility that fans in Philadelphia could be moved to remind Beltran that they beg to differ with his assessment of the NL East. And if so, we know they'll do that in only the most high-class, dignified manner imaginable. Right; sure they will.

"One thing I've noticed about our fans," Myers said. "They're pretty much on top of everything. So I imagine they'll have something to say."

Yeah, we imagine, too. But that's only fair, since Mets fans had something to say in 2007 about Jimmy Rollins' prediction, too. At least, if Rollins' visits to Shea were any indication, the entertainment possibilities this year are pretty much endless.

But several Phillies made the point that Mets fans—and about 99 percent of the rest of the planet—had a huge misconception about Rollins' intentions. What he said may have sounded like trash-talk, but what he intended, in reality, was just to raise the bar of expectations for his *own* team.

"I think he said it because he believed it," Myers said. "We all believed it in our minds, but we're not the outspoken types to come out and say it in the media. He's the type of guy who can do that.

"It's fun that somebody finally said it to where it got out. And it was good for us, because we needed it. We needed it for us, to show we weren't just going to fall back and let everybody run over top of us. It woke everybody up a little bit."

Yep, sure did, and now we have a new wake-up call—for both teams—courtesy of Carlos Beltran. We don't know quite where it's all leading yet. How could we? It's only the third week of February. But we do know that rivalries are the greatest thing in sports. And any time a spectacular new addition to the rivalry annals busts out, that's something to be thankful for—even if you're not someone who's wandering around spring training, trying to capture the magic of pitchers and catchers in a way that, hopefully, justifies the size of your expense account.

"It's gonna be fun," said Shane Victorino. "Put it that way. It's going to be an interesting season. New York Mets 1, Philadelphia Phillies 1. Let's get it on."

Part 2

Five Moments That Defined a Season

The line between winning and losing is thinner than a page of this book, possibly even thinner than an entire book—assuming it's, say, The Life and Times of Fabio Castro.

There are always moments that change everything, moments that determine whether the World Series Express heads north or south. So we now present five moments of truth in the journey of the 2008 Phillies. Had any of them turned out different, let's just say the only people who would have been complaining about the weather in Philadelphia in late October were—who else?—Philadelphians.

The Shortstop Sitteth

The manager and his shortstop don't merely come from different places in life. They practically come from different planets.

Charlie Manuel is 65 years old. He grew up in a little working-class town in the hills of Virginia. He speaks with a vintage *My Name Is Earl* country drawl. He had to sweat his way though 19 pro seasons on two continents just to help his mother support a fatherless household of 11 kids. He made it to home plate in the big leagues only 432 times in all those years.

Jimmy Rollins, on the other hand, just turned 30 four weeks after the 2008 World Series. He grew up on the rough, tough side of Alameda, California. He walks, talks, and plays baseball with a smooth, cocky, hip-hop coolness. He roared into the big leagues, to stay, at 21 years old. He was the MVP of the National League by age 28. He never believed he was required by law to be a slap-hitting, bunt-dropping, little-ball specialist simply because he happened to be a 5'8" shortstop for a living, and many talk-show callers noticed that.

There aren't many walks of life that could bring two men like this so close together. But fate, and their sport, brought Charlie Manuel and

Jimmy Rollins to the same town, assigned them the same mission in life, bonded them in a way only baseball could.

"Jimmy Rollins," said the manager, "is one of my favorite players ever."

What's remarkable about that little quotation is that Charlie Manuel uttered it after a season in which he had to take two dramatic public stands that yanked his favorite shortstop off the field, embarrassed him, and pulled the plug, at least temporarily, on a love affair between Jimmy Rollins and the tough, judgmental city he'd taken years to win over.

Stand No. 1 took place on June 5. Rollins floated a soft pop-up into short left field, flipped his bat away in frustration, and jogged down the first-base line. What he forgot to notice was something kind of important: This ball wasn't going to be caught. So he was only standing on first base, not second, when that ball plunked to rest on the outfield grass. And by the top of the fifth inning, he was shortstop non grata, sentenced to an afternoon of watching the rest of these proceedings from the bench.

That, as it turned out, was only the warm-up act for Stand No. 2. On the final day of a three-day series in New York on July 24, Rollins drove his own car from the Phillies' hotel in Manhattan out to Shea Stadium in Queens. Hit traffic. Didn't arrive until an hour before a 12:10 PM midafternoon game. And had his name scratched off the lineup card for his crime, by court order of Chief Justice Charles Manuel.

Now just so you understand what happened here, this wasn't any old manager disciplining any old player for any old offense. This was a manager whose fans had long ago decided was too soft, too player-friendly, *benching* the reigning MVP, a guy whose whole reputation was built around how hard he plays. And even more stunningly, the manager wasn't doing any of this quietly, behind a locked office door. He was laying it all out there in a way that let the whole world know there was a problem here.

"I didn't do it because I was looking to fight Jimmy Rollins," Manuel would say, many months later. "I didn't do it just to be doing it. I did it because we weren't playing good at the time, and Jimmy's a big part of it. We need Jimmy Rollins. He's our energy."

But it was precisely that energy (or lack thereof) that Manuel was worried about. The manager had grown concerned early in the season that, at times, his team had begun to look way too comfortable, to the point where something was missing. And with Rollins in particular, "It wasn't like I told him about it a couple of times," Manuel said. "I probably told him five or six times, maybe more than that."

And it wasn't only him. In a hitters' meeting one day, Charlie Manuel told his players a story. He told them how much it had always meant to him that the one thing people around baseball kept complimenting him on was the way his team played, its ability to keep its engine revving every day for six months, with no on-off button. But the manager had begun to detect he wasn't seeing the same intensity anymore. So "I said, in that meeting, if they don't start obeying my two rules—hustle and be on time—I was going to pull their ass out of the game," Manuel said. And so, just a few days later, when the MVP himself hit a pop-up and ignored Rule No. 1, there was no other option. It was his butt that got benched.

This time, the first time, Rollins handled it the way MVPs are supposed to handle the tough times. He sat on the bench, rooted for his teammates, then sought out the microphones and refused to blame the manager, the media, the baseball gods, the economy, or the price of premium unleaded. Instead, refreshingly, he pointed the finger directly at himself. "It's my fault," he said afterward. "I can't get mad at him. That's like breaking the law and getting mad that the police show up."

But that wasn't the end of the story. When Rollins rolled into Shea Stadium late a month and a half later, the manager knew he had no choice but to scratch his name off the lineup card a second time. This time, though, the shortstop wasn't so congenial. The term that would better describe him was "ticked off." He marched into the office, told his side of the story, and tried to explain the extenuating circumstances.

And the manager wouldn't buy it. Any of it.

He told Rollins, succinctly, "You should have left earlier." And that was that. It's the manager's philosophy to allow all his players enough space to be themselves, so if the MVP tended to be one of the last players to stroll through the clubhouse doors most days, Charlie Manuel could live with that. But walking in an hour before a game this big? He couldn't live with *that*.

"I'll tell you this," Manuel said. "There's no way in the world I was picking on Jimmy Rollins. If anybody on my team had done that, I'd have done the same thing."

It took the shortstop a while to convince himself of that, though. Took him a while to get over being singled out so publicly for what he thought was a minor offense, perpetrated by those uncooperative New York traffic lights. "We're not going to agree on this one," Rollins told the media mob at Shea that day. "I agreed with him last time, but we're not going to agree on this one."

But ultimately, he got past it. Ultimately, Jimmy Rollins would say, many weeks later, "It's about the team. I've always said it's about the team." And ultimately, the way Charlie Manuel handled those transgressions by his MVP left a lasting imprint on the season, on his clubhouse—and, maybe above all, on the manager's reputation in his own city.

For one thing, he delivered a message that blew his players' comfort zones to smithereens. It told them all that "with Charlie, nobody's above his law," said Greg Dobbs. "It was the right thing to do, and even Jimmy would tell you that. I love Jimmy. Jimmy likes to live life on his own terms, but he's a tremendous person. But this was Charlie's way of reminding us that even superstars need to be whipped into shape every now and then."

Just as important, the superstar who got spanked didn't quit on Charlie Manuel. In fact, it was amazing how fast, after Rollins let off a little steam, the MVP and his manager grew as close as they'd ever been. It isn't every manager who can pull that off, you know. You don't think, for instance, that the people who run the Mets didn't notice the difference between how Jose Reyes handled his 2007 benching by Willie Randolph and how Jimmy Rollins responded to *his* benching by the manager down the turnpike? Heck, yeah, they did. In fact, Mets officials have told their friends in baseball that, in part, it was that contrast that helped convince them they needed a different manager, convinced them they needed someone with the people skills of Charlie Manuel.

"I think that's where all my talks with Jimmy during the course of the season paid off," Manuel said. "When you have those kinds of talks, I think your players understand why you're doing what you do sometimes. He knew how much I pull for him, and he knew how much I think of him as a player. And I think because he knew me and I knew him, he knew why I was doing what I was doing."

But maybe most significant of all, these were two moments that transformed the image of Charlie Manuel in a town that had never totally accepted him—until then.

"I think they liked seeing that I can be tough," Manuel would say, months later. "And there *is* that side of me. I don't think people saw that side of me before—or they didn't want to see that side of me."

"It showed these fans that Charlie cared about winning," said Dallas Green, who, once upon a time, might have been Manuel's No. 1 critic within his own organization. "Yeah, he cares about his players, but he cares about winning, and I think the fans figured that out. Charlie got his players on the same path as him, and he kept it that way…and it was about winning. And I think everybody finally understood that he was the boss."

Not even Dallas Green himself understood that in the beginning. But like so many other longtime Philadelphians, this tough-talking one-time manager of the Phillies learned to look past the country twang and discover what the current manager of the Phillies was really all about. And he wasn't the only one. By October, a man this same town once treated like a bumblehead found himself riding a parade float, holding the World Series trophy, and listening to thousands of people chant his name for four solid hours. It's all been part of the unlikely, even miraculous, metamorphosis of Charlie Manuel.

"I rode on the same parade float as Charlie," said Bill Giles. "I'm pretty sure he could run for mayor right now—and win by about 80 percent."

Brett Myers Visits Scenic Lehigh Valley

Pitchers don't show up on the mound on Opening Day because they bribed the manager, blackmailed the pitching coach, or kidnapped all the other starters. Pitchers show up on the mound on Opening Day because they're carefully chosen to be there, because they've earned the right to be there.

But when the Phillies decided to send Brett Myers to the mound on Opening Day, the universal reaction of just about every single living Philadelphian was, "Yo, why the heck are they pitching *this* guy?"

There was, after all, another starting pitcher on this roster, a gentleman named Cole Hamels. And if Cole Hamels wasn't the clear-cut ace on this team, then the Liberty Bell wasn't cracked and a cheesesteak was considered an official health food. This was not something Charlie Manuel just kind of forgot when it came time to pick his Opening Day starter. The manager might forget to take out the trash once in a while, but he has never forgotten who his ace is. In other words, he sent Brett Myers out there on Opening Day for a reason—a reason he thought was vital to the success of his baseball team: The Phillies needed Brett Myers.

Needed him to get over all his pent-up frustrations from losing his gig as the closer—a job he'd decided was his true calling in life (just ahead of becoming the light-heavyweight champion of the world). Needed him to understand that his place in this rotation was a critical part of the Phillies' equation.

Good theory. Too bad it didn't work out so hot.

On Opening Day—as the Phillies were unfurling a messy 11–6 loss to the Nationals, upholding their long-standing Philadelphia tradition of turning Opening Day into a certifiable local disaster—Myers only made it through five pedestrian innings (five hits, four runs, just two swings and misses). Bad day. Telling day.

Three months later, the Opening-Day starter was 3–9—for a team that had spent a month and a half in first place. He had a 5.84 ERA. He'd won precisely one of his last 13 starts. He'd freely admitted his heart wasn't into starting after discovering the "rock star" joys of bullpen duty the year before. His team had gone a terrifying 1–11 since April 23 when he started—but was winning 63 percent of the time when anybody else started. And it wasn't like this was because of crummy luck, you understand.

Nope. It had slightly more to do with the fact that Brett Myers had allowed 24 homers, 30 doubles, a .551 slugging percentage, and a .907 OPS. Here's how ugly those numbers were: If "Opposing Hitters Facing Brett Myers" were one person, that person would have headed into the All-Star break third in the National League in homers, second in doubles, 10th in slugging, and 12th in OPS—and would have been leading Ryan Braun in all four categories. Uh, that ain't good.

So what's a team like the Phillies supposed to do when its Opening Day starter goes all Chad Ogea on them? They invite him to tour the scenic Lehigh Valley, wearing a shirt that says "Iron Pigs" on the front. Naturally.

No one was too sure of it at the time, but sending Myers to the minor leagues was a truly inspired idea, an idea hatched by the unusual tag team of Phillies assistant GM Ruben Amaro Jr. and Myers' agent, Craig Landis. On the last Sunday in June, Landis called Amaro, his one-time college teammate at Stanford, to ask what would turn out to be one of the pivotal questions of the Phillies' season: What could they do to help Brett Myers get his act back together?

Amaro tossed out a proposal idea he knew Landis and Myers wouldn't want to hear—that it might really help this guy to go back to the minor leagues.

At first, Landis thought, *No way.* The rules said Myers didn't have to go, and, if he didn't want to, the Phillies couldn't make him. But the more the agent thought about it, the more brilliant this concept began to look.

"I'll tell you why I thought maybe it was a good idea," Landis said. "One, he was pitching bad. But more than that, it was getting to him. He was frustrated, probably as much as he'd ever been. He'd lost his swagger. For the first time, he was having doubts about himself. And I didn't see it turning around in the big leagues. He'd hit rock bottom. So I felt like there had to be a change of some kind, because it was bad."

So a few hours later, Landis called Amaro back and told him that he wouldn't stand in the way—but only if Myers was cool with it, too. Except Brett Myers was totally uncool with it. At first, anyway.

The manager called him into the office and laid it out for him. This wasn't punishment, Charlie Manuel told him. They just wanted to help him, the manager said. Manuel tried to frame this request in the most upbeat possible light. He told Myers he still thought he could be a 20-game winner, and he didn't mean winning 20 for the Iron Pigs, either. But "I also said, 'Look, man, we've got to do something, 'cause what we're doing here is not working,'" Manuel said. Finally, the manager wanted to make sure Myers understood something very important: No matter what he decided, he was out of the rotation. There was no way they could start him again, not the way he was pitching. Then he sent Myers out the door to reflect on how to handle the rest of his baseball life.

Brett Myers left the office stunned and hurt and confused. Then he began swirling this scenario around in his head. Talked to his wife. Talked to his agent. Talked to his father, always one of the biggest influences in his life. Thought some more. Talked some more. Remarkably, only one day later, he'd convinced himself he had nothing to lose—as long as the Phillies promised he'd be down there no more than 20 days (so he wouldn't lose any big-league service time) and that he could stay at home between starts. The club agreed. And so began Brett Myers' Excellent Minor League Adventure.

"I knew that I needed to go down and take responsibility for how I was pitching," Myers would say months afterward, knowing how fortuitously his unlikely journey had worked out. "I needed to get it right. And I did."

And one big reason he did was that, in Lehigh Valley, he reconnected with Rod Nichols, one of his first minor-league pitching coaches way back when. They were two men with a bond. And never had that bond meant more to Brett Myers than it did at this perplexing juncture in his career.

"He's kind of always had an insight into how my mechanics were, and he really challenged me mentally and physically, which is good for me," Myers said. "Some of the stuff he says would kind of make me think. And it's not necessarily about pitching or anything like that. He kind of triggers you."

Nobody could have known then that what Nichols triggered in Myers would also trigger the Phillies winning the World Series. But stuff happens. Stuff nobody ever figured on. It's the beauty of sports. So they worked on his fastball. They tweaked his mechanics. But more than any of that, they found a way for Brett Myers to relax, turn off the pressure valve in his brain, and let his ability take over.

Four starts later—two for Lehigh Valley, one for Reading, one for Clearwater—he'd struck out 32 hitters in 30⅓ innings. His fastball had its bounceability back. And Myers had his cocky goofball persona back. He reentered big-league orbit on July 23, in always-sympathetic Shea Stadium. But we should announce here that you won't find any images of that particular outing hanging in the Philly Museum of Art. In the very first inning of his triumphant return, the human reclamation project walked (uh-oh!) *four* hitters—*in a row*. That turned into two runs. In the third inning, in a span of five hitters, he went: walk, hit batter, single, single. That was one more run. Yikes. So how inspired did that minor-league expedition look at *that* point, huh?

But then, out of nowhere, the old Brett Myers showed up. He finished up with two shutout innings. Something clicked inside. "And for the next 10 or 12 starts," said Craig Landis, "he was as good as he'd ever pitched. Ever."

Over the next 10 starts, the Opening-Day starter who had sunk all the way to Farm Land went 7–2 with a dominating 1.56 ERA. Only one pitcher in the National League had a lower ERA in that span. His name was CC Sabathia. So as my buddy Jim Salisbury, of the *Philadelphia Inquirer*, so eloquently put it, if Sabathia was the most important acquisition any NL team made before the July 31 trading deadline, Brett Myers was, in essence, the second-most important.

That run just set the stage for October, where Myers would go on to beat Sabathia in the Phillies' first-round duel with the Brewers, and then beat Chad Billingsley in their NLCS battle with the Dodgers. So now ask yourself this: Do *you* think the Phillies would have won the World Series if Myers hadn't won those battles? We'll never know, obviously. But the correct answer was probably no. So we're not even going to extrapolate here on the minor technicality that Myers somehow hit better in those games than he pitched. (More on that later in this future bestseller.) This is no time to dwell on those goofy technicalities. This is a time to remind you that this was why this man started Opening Day. This was why he was sent on his dramatic safari through the minor-league wilderness. None of this would have been possible had the safari not worked out precisely the way it did.

"I don't think we [could have won] the World Series without him," Charlie Manuel said.

"You know," said Craig Landis, "many things go into winning the World Series. That's just one of those things that goes right along the way."

There's no stat in baseball that measures the way men conquer their inner demons and turn their lives and careers around. But that, when you get right down to it, is what happened here. Just don't ask Brett Myers to explain exactly how it happened.

He sat at an interview-room podium one day in October and listened as someone asked a deep, probing, reflective question about a man whose personal voyage had changed a season: How much, he was asked, had he grown as a person?

"I don't know," Brett Myers chuckled. "I'm still 6'4"."

Moment Three: August 22–25, 2008

Sweep Dreams

On a balmy Monday night in the final week of August, I found myself leaning against the batting cage at Citizens Bank Park. To my right was the hitting coach, Milt Thompson. To my left was the manager, Charlie Manuel. And stepping into that cage for his first batting-practice hacks of the evening was Jimmy Rollins, whose season of turmoil had just taken yet another wrong turn down a dark Philadelphia street.

Only 14 days earlier, Rollins had been a guest on FoxSports' *Best Damn Talk Show Period*, where he'd hung a label on those lovable fans of Philadelphia that turned them even more lovable than usual. That term was "front-runners." As in, "There are times—I might catch some flak for saying this—but, you know, they're front-runners. When you're doing good, they're on your side. When you're doing bad, they're completely against you."

All right, let's do this in two-million part harmony. One, two, three: *Whaaaaaat?* Sheez, there are lots of terms he could have used to describe these people: Demanding. Impatient. Opinionated. Just a tad boo-ish. They all applied. But front-runners? Naaah. Sorry. Doesn't fit.

I'll grant you that these folks may not be the most nurturing fan base on planet Earth. But one thing they're not is front-runners. They show up. They've spent their lifetime paying negotiable cash money to buy tickets for teams that did nothing but break their hearts. And they care—always—whether you're heading for postseason glory or you haven't won a big game since 1957. So while there was a point to be made in there someplace, and a conversation about fan negativity worth having, this was no way to launch it.

So what happened after this show made it onto actual network television? Take a wild guess. Jimmy Rollins—who was already having a rough enough time of it, thanks to those little benching mishaps—abruptly teetered into a realm of Philadelphia sports whipping boys that we don't advise anybody to enter. He wasn't quite T.O., or Rich Kotite, or J.D. Drew. But for a guy who had worked hard to reach the ranks of the Philadelphia beloved, this was one serious plummet in adorability. And it also didn't boost his job-approval rating that, at exactly the same moment, he did something that never helps. He forgot how to hit.

Maybe he figured he'd be better off going incognito, so he trotted out his most vintage Joe Millette impersonation. Nevertheless, as Jimmy Rollins stepped into that batting cage on that August evening two weeks later, he'd gone a terrifying 5-for-50, with one walk and eight strikeouts, since that show aired. Need me to help you with that math? Sorry. Only if you ask all young children to leave the room first. OK, ready? That comes to a .100 batting average and a .135 on-base percentage. Not exactly what this team had in mind for its favorite MVP leadoff man.

But that was all about to change. And somehow, Milt Thompson knew it was about to change. He even made a special point of telling me, with no prompting whatsoever, that it was about to change. And "soon," he said. "Real soon." And why was that? "Because September's coming," the hitting coach said.

What he meant was that, no matter where people may think Rollins' head is located at any given moment, he still cares more about winning than anything else. And September is the month that separates winners from the rest of the population. So what happened? Jimmy Rollins didn't wait for September. That's what.

He reached base five times that night (3-for-3, with a walk and a hit-by-pitch). He got five straight hits the next night. He even became just the second National Leaguer in the last half-century—joining only Pete Rose, on July 26, 1973—to jam five hits, three stolen bases, and a homer into the same game. From that night through the end of the season, the leadoff man would hit .352 with a .439 on-base percentage. And in games in which he scored a run, the Phillies would go 11–4.

So we can look back on that evening for what it really was—the night Jimmy Rollins did what he does best. He turned the key in his team's ignition. He was back. And they were back.

That game finished off a four-game sweep of a Dodgers team that had just swept a four-game series from the Phillies in L.A. earlier in the month. And that, said Charlie Manuel, "kind of started us off. I think we knew we could beat the Dodgers, and we had something to prove."

For the previous two months, they'd lost That Look of a team with the potential to rampage through October. After starting the season 41–28 and building a seven-and-a-half-game lead over the Mets, they'd gone a mediocre 27–31 over the previous nine weeks. They weren't hitting. Their bullpen was beginning to sputter. The Mets were taking charge. And then the Dodgers came to town. Wham. Without warning, the light went back on.

"I just think we got fed up with playing subpar baseball and playing below our capabilities," said Greg Dobbs. "There was a realization, I think, that 'We've gotta get it in gear.' It was like, 'We know we've got more talent than a lot of these teams, so let's start doing something about it.' And we did."

The day after the Dodgers left town, the Mets arrived. All the Phillies did that night was fall behind Pedro Martinez, 7–0—and win—with

Jimmy Rollins looking like he might never make another out and those front-running fans opening their hearts to give him a second chance. All told, starting with that Dodgers game, Rollins went 10-for-his-next-16, with three walks, four extra-base hits, and six RBIs, over the next four games. Amazingly, during his 2007 MVP season, he never had *any* four-game stretches like that.

September was coming. Jimmy Rollins was ready. And so, apparently, was his baseball team.

Moment Four: September 11–14, 2008

Sweet 16 (Again)

Is déjà vu real? Or is it just an illusion? When history seems to repeat itself, is that a trend or a coincidence?

These are questions way too existential to show up in the middle of a book about a baseball team, don't you think? These are lines you'd expect to hear in a Morgan Freeman movie. Or possibly in a *Lost* script.

But the Phillies make you think about these things. How can you not? When a team writes virtually the same mind-blowing ending to the same improbable story two seasons in a row, how do you not wonder? Did it just work out that way? Or was there something more going on here?

Let's refresh your memory. In 2007, with 16 games to play, the Phillies were hopelessly behind the Mets (definition of "hopeless": six and a half games out). Then the schedule brought those Mets to Philadelphia, and craziness happened.

Needing to sweep a three-game series to keep their pulse beating, the Phillies (yep) swept a three-game series. That got the Mets' collapsation avalanche rolling. The Phillies then stampeded through the last two weeks of the season like a team that didn't think it was supposed to lose a game to anybody. Ever. And it was the Phillies who wound up in the playoffs. Whoooah. How'd that happen?

All right, now you can tell Morgan Freeman to cue the spooky music and flash-forward to 2008. Once again, with 16 games left, here were the Phillies, hopelessly behind in both the NL East and wild-card races (the 2008 definition of "hopeless": three and a half games back of the Mets, four behind the Brewers in the wild-card standings). Then the Brewers arrived in their town for a four-game series.

Needing to sweep a four-game series to avoid the intensive-care ward, the Phillies (naturally) swept a four-game series. The Brewers were so spooked, they fired their manager (poor Ned Yost) and barely eked into the postseason. The Phillies? They reached into their transmission box, found that same extra gear they'd stowed away in September 2007, and, well, did it again.

So how do we explain these things, huh? How do we explain a team that wins just about every day when the only way it can keep inhaling and exhaling is to win just about every day? Ya think this stuff just happens? I don't. I think it happens because this team had something going on that I'd like to have a distinguished panel of sports psychologists study for about the next 50 years.

"This team," said Jayson Werth, during that September tear, "is a team of necessity sometimes. If you look back to last year, when we needed to win, we won."

They finished with a 13–4 blitz in 2007. They closed with a 13–3 streak in 2008. What team does that two years in a row, anyway? How is it even possible to do it two years in a row? Well, here's the deal: It isn't. Or at least it wasn't—until this team did it.

I could only find three other teams in history that had back-to-back finishes that good and came in first in either their league, division, or friendly neighborhood wild-card race in both years. One was the 2000–2001 Oakland A's. But in 2001, those A's were 11 games up in the wild-card race when they got rolling. So sorry. Not the same thing. Ditto for the 1998–1999 Braves, a club that never trailed in the NL East at any point in either September. And the only other team I could find was King Kelly's 1891–1892 Boston Beaneaters. But they didn't have to make a mad charge from behind the leader in both those seasons, either. So they're out, too.

Which means the 2007–2008 Phillies are the only team in the history of baseball to have two straight years where they got this hot this late for one basic reason: They had no choice.

"If that," said Greg Dobbs, "doesn't typify this club and the type of men who are on this club...if that doesn't put into focus the type of people we have and what they're really made of, I don't know what would.

"You know that book [by Rick Warren], *The Purpose Driven Life*?'" Dobbs asked. "With us, it was more like *The Purpose-Driven Season*, because it was all about purpose."

I've often thought in the past that when you heard people in sports talk about their sense of purpose, it was usually a convenient, after-the-fact rationalization of what just happened. But after watching this Phillies team close-up, I think that concept, sense of purpose, explains everything. It especially explains 2008. But it was 2007 that laid that groundwork, rearranged the sense-of-purpose genes in all their brains or something. Because this team consciously *felt* like it was reenacting the same script.

"We kept that mind-set," said Charlie Manuel. "When we did it the first time, I think that kind of sent a message that hey, we know we can do it again. And the thing about it that's absolutely unreal is, that's the best we played all year long—in September, when we had to. That's when we played our best baseball. It just goes to show how we look at things—our determination, our focus. And everything we did fell in line."

In 2007, of course, that September hot streak got them to the finish line, but that was that. They celebrated their magical, impossible title a little too hard, enjoyed it a little too much and got bounced out of the postseason faster than you could say, "Kyle Lohse, meet Kaz Matsui." But in 2008, fueled by the lessons they'd learned from their sweeperoo exit the year before, the Phillies got to October feeling more like a team that had merely made it to the starting line. Whereupon they ripped off another streak just like it—an 11–3 swath through October. And when you have those kinds of streaks in October, you don't file them away as trivia.

You file them under history.

The Clincher

For three years, the ghost of Albert Pujols followed Brad Lidge everywhere. To the mound. To the shower. To the video room. To every city in the National League. Possibly even to the convenience store as he stopped for a late-night chili dog. The ghost of Albert Pujols was tough to shake, all right. But then Brad Lidge arrived in Philadelphia in 2008 and found himself stalked by a different set of ghosts—ghosts he wasn't so familiar with:

The ghost of Mitch Williams. The ghost of Jose Mesa. The ghost of Gene Garber. The ghost of Jack Baldschun. The ghosts, in other words, of all those Phillies closers before him who did what a half-century of late-inning Phillies relievers not named Tug McGraw always seemed to do when the games grew large: Self-destruct.

But what was different about this set of ghosts was that it wasn't Lidge himself who was haunted by them. It was all those people in Philadelphia who watched him cruise through a season of perfection— and knew this couldn't possibly be a good thing.

In Philadelphia, you see, closers aren't supposed to be perfect. That would be totally un-Philadelphia-like. Closers are supposed to march in, give up home runs to Joe Carter, give up doubles to Manny Mota, and blow up every dream in your head. In Philadelphia, nobody is supposed to live happily ever after. Isn't that a statute in the City Charter? So as Brad Lidge's save streak began to mount—to 20 in a row, to 30 in a row, to 40 in a row—that voice of doom in every Philadelphian's brain began speaking.

"This is bad," said the voice of doom. "This is dangerous," said the voice of doom. "You know where this is leading," said the voice of doom. It was leading, the voice was 100 percent certain, to one of those classic Philadelphia moments. To a headline that would undoubtedly read: Lidge's First Blown Save Costs Phillies Pennant. The voice of doom could not be silenced. And, amazingly, every Philadelphian could hear it.

Even the chairman of the Phillies could hear it. Couldn't shut it up no matter how hard he tried.

"I kept having nightmares," Bill Giles confessed. "I was having nightmares about Brad Lidge blowing a save in the most critical game of the year."

Which brings us to the fateful afternoon of September 27. Clinch Day. The top of the ninth inning was about to begin. The Phillies were three outs away from clinching the NL East. The familiar sounds of Drowning Pool's "Soldiers" blared through Citizens Bank Park. The closer popped through the bullpen door. Rally towels twirled. The ballpark rattled. And the voice of doom was back.

The closer's save streak was up to 40-for-40. His team was an omnipotent 77–0 when it held a lead after eight innings. The closer had made that possible. Had all games ended after the eighth inning in 2008, the Mets would have won this division by five games. Seriously. That's a fact. Brad Lidge was that important. And that good. He had a 1.84 ERA and an unhittable slider. And now he held a two-run lead against the worst team in baseball, the Washington Nationals. What could possibly happen? Hah. The voice of doom was still yapping.

Lidge struck out the first hitter. Two outs to go. The ballpark vibrated with utter delirium. It was so loud, you could barely hear the voice of doom as it yelled, "It ain't over, ya know!" Darned if that voice wasn't right. The mysterious Roger Bernadina singled. Then the well-traveled Ryan Langerhans walked. Then the world-famous Anderson Hernandez singled in a run. And it sure was getting uncomfortable on the highway to baseball heaven.

The next hitter, Cristian Guzman, bounced *another* single through the middle. But Langerhans froze for just an instant, making sure the ball went through. So he was forced to pull up at third base. The bases were loaded. Loaded. Of course they were.

Lidge tried to soothe his nerves, taking gulps of air so deep he could have held his breath for the next 10 minutes. Now the one dangerous run-producer in this lineup, Ryan Zimmerman, was waiting for him.

The closer wound, fired, and overthrew another slider. Actually bounced it in front of the plate. Then he watched in horror as it hopped past catcher Carlos Ruiz. But here, an astounding, totally un-Philadelphia-esque thing happened: Ruiz flipped off his mask, spun, somehow found the baseball still floating within reach, and snatched it out of the sky. Langerhans was still stuck on third. It was a miracle, this play.

But not as big a miracle as the next play. Zimmerman smoked a ball past the mound that looked like a hit to every trembling human in the park. Obviously, it was heading not just for center field, but for its proper place in Phillies infamy. Obviously, two runs were going to score. Obviously, Lidge's beautiful save streak was going to be defunct. And obviously, another legendary Philadelphia sports disaster was going to scar every eyewitness for at least the next 11,000 years.

Except that isn't how it turned out.

Somehow, Brad Lidge's shortstop materialized behind the bag. Somehow, Jimmy Rollins found a way to dive and skid and scoop up the baseball. Somehow, he then found a way to balance himself on his kneecaps and flip this ball to Chase Utley. And somehow, Utley snapped off the double-play pivot of his lifetime. And somehow, in those four mind-warping seconds, epic Philadelphia heartbreak had turned into a moment of incomprehensible triumph. And the voice of doom was nowhere to be heard.

"I can still remember how I felt when that ball left the bat," Charlie Manuel would say two months later. "I was saying, 'Nooooo.' And then he caught that ball, and they turned that double play, and I said, 'You've gotta be kidding me.'"

Go back through every clinching play in history. Heck, do it right now. I've got a couple of days to kill here while you watch a little video. But I'm telling you before you start cranking up the DVD machine: You're never, ever, going to find a break-out-the-champagne play quite like that. This, friends, was one of the most remarkable clinching plays ever made.

"That guy's a winner," Washington assistant general manager Bob Boone said of Jimmy Rollins that day. "That's a play winning players make."

"I'm a baseball fan just like you," said Phillies reliever Scott Eyre. "And when I think back on the clinching plays I've seen, I can't think of any one that's ever happened like that."

As my friend and ESPN cohort Jerry Crasnick pointed out that day, the normal protocol after games like this is the traditional Pile-Up On Top of the Closer. Not this time. In this game, Lidge and everyone else in uniform began sprinting toward the shortstop.

"He did a lot of screaming," Rollins said of Lidge. "He was like, 'Yeah! Yeah! Yeah!' That's all I remember. I had one ear in his chest and the other ear in Chase's chest, so I just closed my eyes and hoped I didn't get poked in the eye."

Unbelievably, they all emerged unscathed. But that's not why I picked out this game—the next-to-last game on the schedule—as a turning point in this championship season. I picked it out because, in the words of Charlie Manuel, that game and that play "set the whole thing up."

Because Jimmy Rollins made that play, Cole Hamels didn't have to start the next day to save the season. Because he didn't have to start the next day, Hamels was all lined up to start Game 1 against the Brewers. And because Hamels went out and dominated the Brewers in Game 1, it set a million other forces in motion. His team would never trail—not in that series, not in any series through the whole month of October. The rotation would stay in exact place, in exact order, through three straight postseason series, enabling this team to always get the pitching matchup it wanted. One good thing led to another good thing, which led to a month of good things.

Those good things happen to teams that win. Every Philadelphian knows those things haven't happened to the Phillies a whole lot over the potholed life of the franchise. But then, in September and October, they began happening over and over. And the game that brought it all home was this game. The clincher. This was the game that made you wonder. You know all those things that had almost always gone wrong for this team for 125 years? They weren't going wrong all of a sudden.

There's a certain karma that winning teams have. And it was becoming clear that this team had it. It was becoming so apparent that Philadelphians weren't even afraid of the voice of doom anymore.

"For years," said my talk-show pal Mike Missanelli, "the overwhelming reaction to the Phillies has always been this sense of impending doom: 'They're not good enough. They're not gonna spend the dough. Something will go wrong.' And then this happened."

Through the whole month of October, something incredible began to take hold. "There was no sense of panic, at all," Mike Missanelli went on. "Look at the crowd shots. In the past, there was always all that nail-biting. There was always that fear factor. Not this time. For the first time in their lifetimes, these fans knew they had a team that wasn't going to lose."

They had the perfect closer. They had baseballs bouncing precisely where those baseballs needed to bounce. They had Cole Hamels ready when they needed him. There was something going on here, all right. And Philadelphia was about to discover exactly what it was.

Part 3
The National League Division Series

For 25 years, the planets always lined up wrong. For 25 years, whenever something had to happen, the opposite always happened. This was life in Philadelphia for an entire star-crossed quarter-century. Then October 2008 came along. Not only had the Phillies reached into their bag of miracles and made it into the postseason—again—but for once, everything in the heavens seemed to be aligning exactly the way they'd have ordered it up.

Instead of scrambling in as a wild card, they blew by the crumbling Mets and won the NL East. So instead of opening on the road, almost certainly at Wrigley Field, they were home—in a ballpark where they wouldn't lose a single game after September 24. And for their NLDS opponent, they drew a team (the Brewers) they'd just swept in a four-game series only two and a half weeks earlier. Not to mention a team that hadn't played a single post-season game in Cole Hamels' lifetime—and couldn't possibly have been happier just to be still playing. And, finally, there was one more thing to remember: these Brewers were a team that had to go down to the final inning of the final game of the regular season simply to reach this dance floor at all.

And why did that matter so much? Because the Phillies didn't have to do that, didn't have to win on that final day. So they got to save their best pitcher (Hamels) for Game 1 of the postseason—while the Brewers had to send their best pitcher (Mr. Carsten Charles "CC" Sabathia) to the mound that last day merely to survive. Which meant CC couldn't pitch until Game 2 of this series. And when he did pitch, he had to go out there on short rest for the fourth start in a row.

We'll never know how October might have turned out if all those celestial bodies hadn't positioned themselves just right. But Part 3 of this book tells the story of what did happen next, foreshadowing precisely the kind of magic this October had in store.

Game 1: October 1, 2008

It's Never Easy

PHILADELPHIA—In Philadelphia, it's never easy. That's just how life works, how it's always worked, how it always will work. It's been passed down from generation to generation, from Benjamin Franklin to Danny Ozark to Mitch Williams.

So even on the day the Phillies were winning their first meaningful October baseball game since 1993—a 3–1 victory over the Brewers in Game 1 of a fascinating NLDS—this was how it had to end:

With hearts thumping. With rally towels waving. With 45,000 people riding a roller coaster of the senses—never sure if they were one pitch away from elation or a massive coronary.

With eight spectacular, two-hit shutout innings by Cole Hamels receding rapidly into the recesses of an entire city's memory banks. With Brad Lidge, the best closer in baseball in 2008—a man who hadn't blown a save during an entire season—manufacturing more trouble in one inning that Hamels had faced in the previous two and a half hours.

With rain pelting. With winds swirling. With the tying run in scoring position. With a Game 2 meeting with CC Sabathia looking more ominous every second.

And then, just as disaster seemed clearly ready to descend, Lidge reached back for his 35th pitch of a harrowing inning, blew a 93-mile-an-hour scorchball past Corey Hart for a game-ending strikeout and sealed his craziest save of the year, not to mention his biggest.

Game 1 in a best-of-five series is always humongous. But when the Game 2 starter is the omnipotent Carsten Charles Sabathia, it's doubly humongous.

And that's where the Phillies found themselves. Maybe they hadn't gone 26 years between postseason wins like the Brewers. But 15 years is longer than you think. Before Game 1, the Yankees had piled up 78 postseason victories just since the Phillies' *last* postseason victory.

So a whole bunch of those people reaching for their blood-pressure medication in the seats had good reason to think that last out would never come. And even those eight other Phillies out there on the field with Lidge were beginning to waver.

"I think he read too much into me saying it wouldn't be the Philly way if things weren't difficult," laughed Jimmy Rollins after the first postseason win of his lifetime. "I don't think he got the memo when I said, 'I take that back.'"

Rollins then turned and looked deep into the lenses of the 97 cameras pointed directly at his face.

"Hopefully," the shortstop said, "he'll be watching the news tonight. 'Brad, to all the cameras, it's okay to go 1-2-3.'"

Oh, it's okay, all right. But it wouldn't be very Philadelphian. In Philadelphia, there's no such thing as a routine postseason victory, even on a day when the local starting pitcher gives them eight innings of sheer unhittability.

And for eight innings, that's what Cole Hamels was in Game 1— unhittable.

He didn't allow a hit until Hart (1 for 14 lifetime, with six strikeouts against him) singled with two outs in the fifth—the longest postseason no-hit bid by any Phillies pitcher since Jim Lonborg went two outs farther in Game 2 of the 1976 NLCS.

"Whenever you get your first hit…in the fifth," said Hart later, "it's usually not a good day."

Yep. No kidding. Over eight innings, the Brewers pieced together exactly two hits, three base runners, and one runner in scoring position. Hamels had his best David Copperfield disappearing change-up going. And for the eight innings he was out there, the Brewers couldn't touch it.

"He had good stuff, man," said Milwaukee leadoff man Mike Cameron, who drew his team's one walk off Hamels. "He had great deception on his pitches.… You try to be patient, but at the same time he has pretty good command of his change-up. I think he got comfortable, and he kind of fed off the energy of the ballpark."

In fact, though, Hamels said afterward that that's exactly what he was trying *not* to do. He learned his lesson a year ago, when he uncharacteristically walked four hitters in a painful Game 1 NLDS loss to the Rockies. And this time around, he said, his goal was to ignore that thunder erupting from the seats and stay cool.

"I knew the importance of the game," Hamels said. "And it's something where, because of last year, I learned what it really takes in trying to…kind of mellow out, not to have that sort of excitement where you can't really control everything."

It wasn't just last year's disappointment that delivered that powerful message. It was also this pitching staff's resident Yoda—veteran left-handed sage Jamie Moyer.

Moyer said he approached Hamels in the trainer's room before this game for a little chat about how to deal with postseason madness.

Cole Hamels is applauded by fans as he steps into the dugout after the third inning of Game 1 of the National League Division Series against the Milwaukee Brewers on October 1, 2008.

"I told him, 'It's the playoffs, yes. But you still have to go about it the same,'" Moyer said. "I said, 'Just remember you're the same person. Don't lose sight of why you're here or what you've done to get here.'"

What Hamels did to get here was have himself a season that could easily have elevated him into the Cy Young debate with a little luck and better run support. He finished in the top three in the league in shutouts, opponent batting average, and innings pitched—and in the top six in ERA, strikeouts, and quality starts.

But thanks to 10 starts in which he gave up two earned runs or fewer and didn't win, all that brilliance translated into just 14 wins. So heading into this series, Hamels found himself lost in the giant shadow of that other left-handed dominator, Sabathia.

In Game 1, however, it was Cole Hamels' turn to take the October stage. And there's nowhere else he would rather have been. This is a guy who aspires to more, who aspires to greatness, who aspires to take the ball on days like this and pitch masterpieces just like this one. So this game was a giant step in his journey toward acehood.

"This was just another hurdle for him to overcome," Moyer said. "At this age [24], to gain this experience is huge. But not just for him. For everyone in this clubhouse.

"Today was a huge day for us, with him on the mound. For this group of players, most of us were here last year, and remember what it felt like to go 0–3 [against the Rockies]. So to go out today and win that first game—that's a big victory for this clubhouse, because most of these guys have never won a postseason game."

In 2007 Hamels was outdueled by Jeff Francis in Game 1, and his team never recovered. At the time, Rollins said, they didn't see that 1–0 hole as a big deal. They soon found out otherwise.

"The next thing we knew, it was 2–0," he said. "And the next thing we knew, we were going home."

But this time around, this was a group with bigger aspirations. So they knew what this one meant. And the man on the mound almost made it easy—with the help of a couple of Brewers defensive glitches that fueled a three-run third inning.

So after eight innings, the Phillies held a theoretically comfortable 3–0 lead. And Hamels was just three outs away from what would have been the first two-hit complete-game shutout pitched by *any* pitcher in a postseason Game 1 since Whitey Ford in the 1961 World Series.

But Hamels' pitch count also had reached 101. And the Phillies looked ahead to the possibility that they could need him to come back on short rest for Game 4. So in marched Lidge to start the ninth.

"That's why he's standing down there," said manager Charlie Manuel, of his closer. "That's his job, too. And he's been perfect."

He sure had. But it was amazing how fast that perfection—and those 41 straight saves—seemed 100 percent irrelevant.

Lidge whiffed Mike Cameron for the first out. But then a Ray Durham single, a Ryan Braun double, and a Chase Utley error turned it into a 3–1 nail-chomper.

Lidge did win an epic eight-pitch mano-a-mano with Prince Fielder, punching him out on a full-count fastball for the second out. But a walk to J.J. Hardy and a wild pitch put runners on second and third for Hart.

They dueled to 2-and-2. Lidge took a huge breath and stared at his shoes. Towels waved. Pulses raced. Lidge fired. Hart swung and missed. And the Phillies' date with CC didn't seem so life-threatening anymore.

Rollins headed straight for Lidge. "You don't have to make it *that* interesting," the shortstop said. "What happened to those guys who come out and go 1-2-3?"

"It would be nice...but I've never been that type of pitcher," Lidge replied.

"Well, it's never too late to start," Rollins chuckled.

As you may recall, Lidge has had his share of October adventures. So when he was asked if he was aware that he'd just caused 2 million heart attacks, he almost sounded guilty.

"I'll have to buy everyone some Bayer [aspirin] and Advil," he quipped, "or whatever eases the heart."

Those hearts only had 24 hours to gear up for Sabathia in Game 2. But hey, that just added to the fun.

"I know it's CC, but nobody knows what's going to happen tomorrow," said Jamie Moyer, his sage cap back in place. "We'll just have to wait till tomorrow and find out."

And, as usual, how right he was.

NL Division Series, Game 1,
October 1, 2008, at Philadelphia
Phillies 3, Brewers 1

Milwaukee	AB	R	H	RBI	BB	SO	LOB	AVG
Cameron, CF	3	0	0	0	1	2	0	.000
Hall, 3B	3	0	0	0	0	1	2	.000
b-Durham, PH	1	1	1	0	0	0	0	1.000
Braun, LF	4	0	1	0	0	1	2	.250
Fielder, 1B	4	0	0	0	0	3	1	.000
Hardy, SS	3	0	0	0	1	0	0	.000
Hart, C, RF	4	0	1	0	0	1	2	.250
Weeks, 2B	2	0	0	0	0	2	1	.000
Villanueva, P	0	0	0	0	0	0	0	.000
a-Gwynn, PH	1	0	0	0	0	0	0	.000
Parra, P	0	0	0	0	0	0	0	.000
Mota, P	0	0	0	0	0	0	0	.000
Kendall, C	3	0	0	0	0	2	0	.000
Gallardo, P	1	0	0	0	0	0	0	.000
Stetter, P	0	0	0	0	0	0	0	.000
Counsell, 2B	2	0	1	0	0	0	0	.500
Totals	31	1	4	0	2	12	8	

Philadelphia	AB	R	H	RBI	BB	SO	LOB	AVG
Rollins, SS	4	0	1	0	0	1	2	.250
Werth, RF	4	0	0	0	0	3	3	.000
Utley, 2B	4	1	1	2	0	0	0	.250
Howard, 1B	1	0	0	0	3	1	0	.000
Burrell, LF	2	0	0	0	1	0	1	.000
Bruntlett, LF	1	0	1	0	0	0	0	1.000
Victorino, CF	2	0	0	1	2	0	2	.000
Feliz, 3B	4	0	0	0	0	0	6	.000
Ruiz, C	3	1	1	0	0	0	0	.333
Hamels, P	2	1	0	0	0	2	0	.000
Lidge, P	0	0	0	0	0	0	0	.000
Totals	27	3	4	3	6	7	14	

a-Bunted out for Villanueva in the 8th. b-Singled for Hall in the 9th.

BATTING
2B: Braun (1, Lidge).
TB: Durham; Braun 2; Hart, C; Counsell.
Runners left in scoring position, 2 out: Braun; Hart, C 2.
Team LOB: 5.

FIELDING
E: Weeks (1, missed catch).
DP: (Hardy-Fielder).

BATTING
2B: Utley (1, Gallardo).
TB: Rollins; Utley 2; Bruntlett; Ruiz.
RBI: Utley 2 (2), Victorino (1).
2-out RBI: Utley 2; Victorino.
Runners left in scoring position, 2 out: Feliz 4.
S: Hamels.
GIDP: Burrell.
Team LOB: 7.

BASERUNNING
SB: Victorino (1, 2nd base off Mota/Kendall).

FIELDING
E: Utley (1, missed catch).

Milwaukee	IP	H	R	ER	BB	SO	HR	ERA
Gallardo (L, 0-1)	4.0	3	3	0	5	3	0	0.00
Stetter	0.2	0	0	0	0	1	0	0.00
Villanueva	2.1	0	0	0	0	3	0	0.00
Parra	0.2	1	0	0	1	0	0	0.00
Mota	0.1	0	0	0	0	0	0	0.00

Philadelphia	IP	H	R	ER	BB	SO	HR	ERA
Hamels (W, 1-0)	8.0	2	0	0	1	9	0	0.00
Lidge (S, 1)	1.0	2	1	1	1	3	0	9.00

WP: Lidge; IBB: Howard (by Gallardo); Pitches-strikes: Gallardo 75-37, Stetter 12-7, Villanueva 24-18, Parra 15-8, Mota 7-5, Hamels 101-67, Lidge 35-19 Groundouts-flyouts: Gallardo 4-5, Stetter 1-0, Villanueva 1-3, Parra 2-0, Mota 0-1, Hamels 8-7, Lidge 0-0; Batters faced: Gallardo 20, Stetter 2, Villanueva 7, Parra 4, Mota 1, Hamels 27, Lidge 6; Inherited runners-scored: Mota 2-0; Umpires: HP: Dana DeMuth. 1B: Mark Wegner. 2B: Brian Runge. 3B: Fieldin Culbreth. LF: Jim Joyce. RF: Paul Nauert

Weather: 72 degrees, cloudy; Wind: 9 mph, Out to RF; T: 2:39; Att: 45,929.

Useless
Information

- In Game 1 of the postseason, Cole Hamels spun off eight innings of two-hit, no-run, nine-strikeout baseball. The Phillies hadn't had a start like that in the *regular* season in any of their previous 699 games (dating all the way back to a Brett Myers masterpiece on August 8, 2004).

- On the other hand, suppose we just ask: When was the last time a Phillies starter pitched at least eight shutout innings in a postseason game? The answer to that question: Exactly one postseason win ago—in Curt Schilling's complete-game shutout of the Blue Jays in Game 5 of the 1993 World Series.

- The Phillies went 5–17 after June 12 in games in which they didn't homer, but they won their first game of the postseason even though they forgot to homer.

- Shane Victorino's bases-loaded walk, off Yovani Gallardo, gave the Phillies their third run of the third inning. Before that, naturally, Gallardo had never walked *any* hitter with the bases loaded in his career, and Victorino hadn't drawn a bases-loaded walk in his last 955 trips to the plate, counting the postseason.

- Brad Lidge needed 35 pitches to save this game. He hadn't thrown 35 pitches in any of his last 138 saves (postseason or regular-season). Last time he did it: Game 3 of the 2004 NLCS, in a 42-pitch, six-out save against the Cardinals.

Game 2: October 2, 2008

CC You Later

PHILADELPHIA—Wait. What just happened here?

That couldn't have been the great CC Sabathia serving up that shocking Ruben Quevedo impression in Game 2, on the biggest night of his Brewers career. Could it? Impossible.

This was going to be CC's stage, CC's moment. Everybody knew that.

This was going to be the night he single-handedly saved the Brewers' first visit to October since the Reagan administration, evened the NLDS, and then took the controls of the team charter and flew it back to Milwaukee all by himself. All while serving steaks to his teammates that he'd just grilled up for them personally—to order, of course. It was all scripted for him, all laid out by the baseball gods with perfect precision. If only that was how October works.

Instead, October served up the most disastrous outing of Sabathia's Brewers career—all 18 starts of it.

What October served up was 3⅔ tortuous innings by a man who started the night with a 1.65 ERA in this uniform. Five runs. Six hits—every darned one of them an extra-base hit. One grand slam to a 160-pound Hawaiian (Shane Victorino). Four walks. And 98 exhausting pitches—19 of them just to the opposing pitcher (Brett Myers)—in an outing that didn't even last four innings.

What October served up, most of all, was a devastating 5–2 loss to the Phillies that left the Brewers buried, two games to zilch, with their man CC not scheduled to start for them again until a Game 5 that never came.

This was not how those Milwaukee Brewers laid it out, not how anybody outside the 215 area code saw this night unfolding. But that's life in October. What's scripted and what happens are often two different things.

"No one's perfect," said Phillies closer Brad Lidge, a man who ought to know. "That's just how baseball is.... Everybody in baseball is talking about how great CC Sabathia is. And everybody in baseball is just expecting it to be 1–1 after today. But that's baseball. It's not that easy."

For his three months as a Brewer, however, the amazing CC had made it look almost as easy as playing catch on the beach. He didn't lose for 14 starts. He went nine innings any old time his team needed him to. He was like a behemoth out of a 1914 time warp, launching 122 pitches on short rest and acting like it was no big whoop.

So why *wouldn't* the world have expected him to rise up—in his fourth straight trip to the mound on three days' rest—and rescue the franchise one more time? That's what superheroes do. And that's exactly what he had been doing for months, over and over and over again.

But when he was asked after this game if people expect too much of men like him on nights like this, Sabathia shook his head firmly.

"No," he answered, "because I expect that out of myself. And this is where I need to be. This is the situation I want to be in. This is the situation I *need* to be in. And I needed to come out here and pitch a good game tonight. And I didn't do that. So you can blame this loss squarely on me."

That's not the same thing as saying you can blame this loss *only* on him, of course. His team's offense, after all, had mustered seven hits in two games—just three in this game off Myers and the back end of the Phillies bullpen.

But part of being a great player is accepting responsibility when things go wrong. So CC Sabathia accepted every last ounce of it—because no one needed to explain to him what he was supposed to do on this night, but didn't.

There were a million excuses out there to be made. Sabathia made none of them. He was the first pitcher since 2003 (Danny Graves) to make four straight starts on three days' rest, according to the Elias Sports Bureau. He was the first in 16 years (since John Smoltz in 1992) to do that in a stretch that included *any* starts in the postseason. But when he was offered that alibi, he wanted no part of it.

"I don't feel like starting on three days' rest had anything to do with it, or anything like that," he said. "I just think tonight I didn't make pitches when I needed to."

Even in the other clubhouse, though, they didn't see it that way.

"I know he's a horse. I know he's their go-to guy. But he's got to be tired," said Phillies reliever Scott Eyre. "Guys just don't do what he's done anymore. They don't gear pitchers to pitch on three days' rest anymore—especially not as much as he's done it."

Whether he was running on fumes or not, however, this was a night unlike just about any Sabathia had spent on a mound in his career. And he'd been out there 258 times before this, counting the postseason. But here's what made this game such a shocker:

- This is a man who gave up six earned runs in the entire month of August. He gave up five in the second inning just in a span of *five hitters.*
- This is a man who had allowed one extra-base hit in his previous three starts on short rest combined. He allowed three extra-base hits in this game just in his first trip through the batting order, then served up that crushing Victorino slam two hitters later.

- Only four other times in those 258 starts had Sabathia given up six extra-base hits in one game. But he'd never had a start where he gave up all those extra-base hits and not one measly single.
- And he'd never made a start in which he gave up this many extra-base hits without at least getting through the fourth inning.

Nights like this happen to everybody sooner or later. But for Sabathia and this team, which he'd just lugged to October like a human tow truck, this wasn't exactly the time they had in mind.

For three months, said Craig Counsell, Sabathia had been the ultimate security blanket. For three months, Counsell said, "Your feeling when you've got your ace on the mound is that you know he's going to give you a chance. And you know it's going to be tough on the other team. That's what it's been like. It's been a great feeling. But today, Victorino got him. He put a good swing on a pitch, and he got him. It happens."

Oh, it happens, sure. But it was the way it all happened that was so stunning. Because the hitter who changed everything was a guy who, by his own admission, is "a terrible hitter."

Shane Victorino follows his second-inning grand slam against the Brewers in Game 2 of the National League Division Series on October 2, 2008.

That man is Brett Myers. And Albert Pujols Jr. he's not. He went 4-for-58 (.069) at the plate in the regular season. Over the last three years, he was 6 for his last 127 (.047). And while he was a .116 lifetime hitter, let the record show he hadn't actually topped .100 since 2005.

So what happened when Myers stepped in to face Sabathia in the second inning was one of those eerie, unexplained phenomena, kinda like Stonehenge. They'll be doing documentaries on this on the SciFi Channel any day now.

Sabathia jumped ahead of him, 0-and-2. Next thing they both knew, Myers was fouling off one unhittable pitch after another, the largest crowd in Citizens Bank Park history was apoplectic, Sabathia was heaving his ninth pitch of the at-bat—and (did this really happen?) leaving it low for ball four.

And this game seemed to turn right there. Four pitches later, Sabathia had walked Jimmy Rollins to load the bases. And four pitches after that, he'd hung a 1-and-2 cutter to Victorino, watched it sail into a sea of rally towels, and pivoted in frustration as the home team's ballpark erupted in utter bedlam.

It was 5–1, Phillies. And it was such a shocking, surreal moment that even Victorino said that as he was roaring around the bases, he asked himself, *Did that really happen?*

Good question. It was the first grand slam in Phillies postseason history. It was the first grand slam in the history of Shane Victorino's lifetime. And it was the second slam ever surrendered by CC—in a career in which he has faced more than 7,000 hitters. So we're still not sure it really happened.

"That was a big, big hit," Rollins said, "because it made that mountain they've got to climb just a little higher."

The Phillies never did score again off Sabathia. But they made him sweat for 10 more hitters, thumping two more doubles, getting four of those last 10 hitters on base, and getting one more improbable 10-pitch at-bat out of the suddenly inexhaustible Brett Myers.

Before this night, Sabathia had faced 58 pitchers in his career. They'd gone 4-for-49 against him, with 28 strikeouts and one walk. Not one of those pitchers had ever extended an at-bat against him beyond seven pitches.

Myers, meanwhile, had never had a 10-pitch at-bat in his career—against anybody. But he had one on this night. Against CC Sabathia. Is this sport insane, or what?

Asked if he was worried about Myers taking his job as leadoff man—after grinding through those 19 pitches in two at-bats—Rollins laughed, "Nah, he doesn't have enough speed. If he gets on, he's not going to be able to steal any bags. So I think I'll be safe there."

What looked safer, however, was the two-games-to-zero lead the Phillies had just taken. Since the Division Series went to its current 2–2–1 format in 1999, 21 previous teams had taken a 2–0 lead. Only three of them lost the series—the 2003 and 2001 A's (against the Red Sox and Yankees, respectively) and the 1999 Indians (against the Red Sox).

So while nothing was impossible, especially with the Brewers heading home, their next two starting pitchers—Dave Bush and Jeff Suppan—went winless in four regular-season starts against the Phillies, allowing 39 base runners in 22⅔ innings. And the Brewers would need to win games started by both of them just to get their main man CC back on the mound one more time.

Those odds weren't good. But if it was any consolation for the Milwaukee Brewers, they could look at it this way: The odds couldn't be any worse than the odds of CC Sabathia becoming the second pitcher in postseason history (along with Darryl Kile in the 2000 NLCS) to give up six extra-base hits without getting out of the fourth inning.

Division Series, Game 2, October 2, 2008, at Philadelphia
Phillies 5, Brewers 2

Milwaukee	AB	R	H	RBI	BB	SO	LOB	AVG
Cameron, CF	4	0	0	0	0	1	1	.000
Durham, 2B	3	1	0	0	1	1	1	.250
Braun, LF	4	0	2	0	0	0	0	.375
Fielder, 1B	3	0	0	0	1	0	2	.000
Hardy, SS	3	1	1	1	1	0	0	.167
Hart, C, RF	3	0	0	0	0	0	4	.143
Counsell, 3B	4	0	0	1	0	1	1	.167
Kendall, C	3	0	0	0	0	0	0	.000
Sabathia, P	1	0	0	0	0	0	0	.000
Stetter, P	0	0	0	0	0	0	0	.000
a-Gwynn, PH	1	0	0	0	0	1	0	.000
McClung, P	0	0	0	0	0	0	0	.000
Gagne, P	0	0	0	0	0	0	0	.000
b-Weeks, PH	1	0	0	0	0	0	0	.000
Torres, P	0	0	0	0	0	0	0	.000
Totals	30	2	3	2	3	4	9	

Philadelphia	AB	R	H	RBI	BB	SO	LOB	AVG
Rollins, SS	4	1	2	0	1	0	3	.375
Victorino, CF	4	1	3	4	1	0	0	.500
Utley, 2B	4	0	0	0	1	3	2	.125
Howard, 1B	3	0	0	0	1	3	4	.000
Burrell, LF	3	0	0	0	1	1	2	.000
Madson, P	0	0	0	0	0	0	0	.000
Romero, P	0	0	0	0	0	0	0	.000
Lidge, P	0	0	0	0	0	0	0	.000
Werth, RF	4	1	2	0	0	0	3	.250
Feliz, 3B	4	1	1	1	0	1	2	.125
Ruiz, C	3	0	0	0	1	0	1	.167
Myers, P	2	1	1	0	1	0	0	.500
a-Dobbs, PH	1	0	0	0	0	1	0	.000
Bruntlett, LF	0	0	0	0	0	0	0	1.000
Totals	32	5	9	5	7	9	17	

a-Struck out for Stetter in the 5th. b-Reached on error for Gagne in the 8th.

a-Struck out for Myers in the 7th.

BATTING
2B: Braun (2, Myers), Hardy (1, Myers).
TB: Braun 3; Hardy 2.
RBI: Hardy (1), Counsell (1).
Runners left in scoring position, 2 out: Fielder.
GIDP: Hart, C.
Team LOB: 5.

BATTING
2B: Victorino 2 (2, Sabathia, McClung), Werth 2 (2, Sabathia, Sabathia), Feliz (1, Sabathia), Rollins (1, Sabathia).
HR: Victorino (1, 2nd inning off Sabathia, 3 on, 2 out).
TB: Rollins 3; Victorino 8; Werth 4; Feliz 2; Myers.
RBI: Feliz (1), Victorino 4 (5).
2-out RBI: Victorino 4.
Runners left in scoring position, 2 out: Howard 3; Feliz; Rollins 2; Werth.
Team LOB: 10.

BASERUNNING
SB: Victorino 2 (3, 2nd base off Sabathia/Kendall, 3rd base off Sabathia/Kendall), Rollins (1, 3rd base off Sabathia/Kendall), Werth (1, 3rd base off Sabathia/Kendall).
CS: Rollins (1, 2nd base by Torres/Kendall).

FIELDING
E: Rollins (1, fielding).
DP: (Myers-Ruiz-Howard).

Milwaukee	IP	H	R	ER	BB	SO	HR	ERA
Sabathia (L, 0-1)	3.2	6	5	5	4	5	1	12.27
Stetter	0.1	0	0	0	0	1	0	0.00
McClung	2.0	2	0	0	3	1	0	0.00
Gagne	1.0	0	0	0	0	1	0	0.00
Torres	1.0	1	0	0	0	1	0	0.00

Philadelphia	IP	H	R	ER	BB	SO	HR	ERA
Myers (W, 1-0)	7.0	2	2	2	3	4	0	2.57
Madson (H, 1)	0.2	1	0	0	0	0	0	0.00
Romero (H, 1)	0.1	0	0	0	0	0	0	0.00
Lidge (S, 2)	1.0	0	0	0	0	0	0	4.50

IBB: Victorino (by Sabathia), Howard (by McClung), Fielder (by Myers); HBP: Hart, C (by Myers); Pitches-strikes: Sabathia 98-55, Stetter 4-3, McClung 33-17, Gagne 15-9, Torres 14-7, Myers 94-56, Madson 11-8, Romero 1-1, Lidge 12-8; Groundouts-flyouts: Sabathia 3-3, Stetter 0-0, McClung 1-4, Gagne 1-1, Torres 0-1, Myers 10-7, Madson 1-1, Romero 1-0, Lidge 0-3; Batters faced: Sabathia 21, Stetter 1, McClung 11, Gagne 3, Torres 3, Myers 26, Madson 4, Romero 1, Lidge 3; Inherited runners-scored: Stetter 3-0, Romero 2-0; Umpires: HP: Mark Wegner. 1B: Brian Runge. 2B: Fieldin Culbreth. 3B: Jim Joyce. LF: Paul Nauert. RF: Dana DeMuth; Weather: 61 degrees, partly cloudy; Wind: 14 mph, L to R; T: 3:00; Att: 46,208.

Useless
Information

- What got into Brett Myers? In back-to-back trips to the plate, he had a nine-pitch at-bat and a 10-pitch at-bat against CC Sabathia. Before that, according to the Elias Sports Bureau, he'd only had three at-bats of nine pitches or more in his whole career, in 390 regular-season plate appearances.

- Shane Victorino's grand slam off Sabathia broke this game open. Victorino had never hit a regular-season slam, of course. And the Phillies hadn't hit one in any of their previous 61 postseason games in franchise history.

- Victorino was the first player in history—any team's history—to cram a home run, two doubles, and two stolen bases into one postseason game.

- The Phillies got six hits off Sabathia—and they were all extra-base hits. No pitcher had ever given up that many hits in a postseason game without at least one of them being a single.

- The Phillies did something in Games 1 and 2 that they hadn't done in their last 1,099 regular-season games—they got back-to-back games in which their starting pitchers worked at least seven innings and gave up no more than two hits. Last time two Phillies starters did that in consecutive games in the regular season: May 9 and 10, 2002 (by Randy Wolf and Vicente Padilla).

The Walking History Museum

MILWAUKEE—For some reason, the world always seems to forget about Jamie Moyer when the topic turns to the walking history museums of baseball.

Greg Maddux always comes up. Randy Johnson always comes up. Tom Glavine tends to nudge his way into these conversations. Heck, you might even hear names like Mike Timlin or Kenny Rogers or Tim Wakefield before someone gets around to saying, "Hey, what about Jamie Moyer?"

But coming right up in Game 3 in Milwaukee, the Phillies' 45-year-old ageless virtuoso was about to head for the mound at Miller Park with a chance to do something no 45-year-old starting pitcher had ever done before: Win the clinching game of a postseason series.

He was 45 days away from his 46th birthday. His team held a two-games-to-nada lead over the Brewers. So Moyer had the opportunity to seal a postseason series for a franchise that hadn't exactly perfected that art. The Phillies have been around for 126 seasons now—and had won just four of those postseason series in all that time.

But Jamie Moyer also had another opportunity—the opportunity to hold history in his hands. All kinds of history, in fact:

- He had a chance to become the oldest starting pitcher to win a postseason clincher—by *five years*. The current record-holder, according to baseball-reference.com, is Curt Schilling, who was 40 years, 327 days old when he won Game 3 of last year's ALDS sweep for the Red Sox.

- Moyer also was attempting to become the oldest starting pitcher to win any kind of postseason game—by more than two years. Roger Clemens was 43 years, 72 days old when he beat the Cardinals in Game 3 of the 2005 NLCS. Clemens, incidentally, is the only 43-year-old starter ever to win a postseason game—not to mention the only 42-year-old.

- And, finally, Moyer had the opportunity to become the oldest pitcher—starter or reliever—to win a postseason game. Dennis Martinez still holds that distinction, by vulturing a win in relief in the 1998 NLCS (a game in which he threw exactly three pitches), at 43 years, 150 days old. The only other 43-year-olds to win a postseason game in relief were Dolf Luque, in the 1933 World Series, and Clemens, in that madcap 18-inning NLDS game between the Astros and Braves in 2005. Both Luque and Clemens, by the way, won clinching games—but not as starters.

So now it was Jamie Moyer's turn. He's a one-hour History Channel special waiting to happen. But as his rendezvous with history approached, Moyer made it clear he would rather pitch than reflect.

"I probably haven't had any chance to look back," he said, the day before this game, "because I choose not to take that opportunity to look back at it right now. I feel like I need to take advantage of the moment.

"This is a great opportunity to pitch, period. And...to me, at this stage, it's an honor to come here every day just to put the uniform on, just today to come here to work out. I look at that as a huge honor."

But when you talk to the men who play with this guy, you get the sense that they're the ones who feel honored to play with him, not the other way around.

"Jamie, he's tremendous," said Geoff Jenkins. "He's 100 [years old], and he just keeps doing it.... Obviously, I've played against Jamie for a number of years and kind of seen him. But now that I've actually played with him and [gotten] a chance to see his work ethic, how he carries himself, how professional, how he's helping out the other guys on the team, the other pitchers, he's just as valuable when he's *not* pitching as when he is pitching."

If you watch a Phillies game—any Phillies game—we can almost guarantee that sooner or later, the TV cameras will zero in on the Phillies' dugout. And somebody will be locked in deep conversation with Jamie Moyer. On the art of pitching, on the art of professionalism, or on just about anything in between.

He holds a place on his team that's utterly unique—a fascinating cross between Warren Spahn and Gandhi. Jamie Moyer draws teammates to him like a giant magnetic force—to watch and to listen.

"I think those are the things that you really don't see, how much he helps the guys the days that he's not pitching," Jenkins said. "So that makes him more valuable than a guy that just goes out there every fifth day and throws the ball and just doesn't really care about the other guys."

Moyer is well aware of how much his mentoring means to his teammates—especially the young pitchers who never tire of soaking up his wisdom: Cole Hamels, Kyle Kendrick, J.A. Happ.

Once upon a time, though, Moyer was the guy searching for that wisdom. When he begins dropping the names of some of the men he has

Moyer Moves Forward

Jamie Moyer is so open-minded, he'll even do something completely sacrilegious—tap the hitters for knowledge.

"I think you can learn a lot by talking to a hitter…and to me, that's the game," he said. "As a player, you've got to want to learn. You've got to want to continue to get better, because my feeling is, if you become stagnant, you start to go backwards."

sought it from over the years, it is clear just how long he's been around now: Rick Sutcliffe, Nolan Ryan, Charlie Hough, Fernando Valenzuela.

At one point his manager, Charlie Manuel, mentioned Gil Hodges' infamous struggles in the 1952 World Series (0-for-21). Moyer couldn't resist the temptation. "I think I faced Gil Hodges in that Series," he quipped.

At another point, though, Moyer even seemed to startle himself when he tossed Valenzuela's name into the conversation.

"I know I'm aging myself a little bit," he said after that Fernando-mania reference. "But age doesn't matter at this point."

Well, it doesn't seem to matter much to *him*, anyway.

This may be a guy with a lot to teach and share away from the mound. But, oh, by the way, those days he throws the ball have worked out pretty well, too.

Not too many people have noticed that it was Jamie Moyer—the oldest pitcher in baseball—who led a first-place team in wins (with 16). And that makes Moyer the first 45-year-old to win at least 10 games and lead his team in wins since Satchel Paige in 1952.

Those 16 wins are also a modern record for a non-knuckleballer his age. Only Phil Niekro, who won 16 for the '85 Yankees at age 46, was older at the time of his 16-win season.

And speaking of Niekro, he's now the only pitcher in the last 75 years who won more games (121) after turning 40 than the 82 Jamie Moyer had won by the end of the 2008 season. Just in 2008 alone, Moyer passed quite an array of names on that Most Wins After 40 list—blowing by Clemens (66), Hough (67), Ryan (71), and Spahn (75).

But for everything that Moyer *had* done, there was still something missing. He owned just two postseason wins—including the clinching game in the 2001 ALDS. And he had never pitched in a World Series, even missing that opportunity when he was the ace on a team that won 116 games (the '01 Mariners).

Asked how hard it was not to think about how close he might be, Moyer replied, "I don't find it difficult at all, because, No. 1, I haven't been there. So I don't know what that excitement is. I don't know what that feeling is. If we don't win tomorrow or win this series, I'll never know. So to me, the focus is on tomorrow."

As he focused on Game 3, he wouldn't notice, wouldn't even care, how many eyes would be focused on him. But it would be more than he thought, because this was one start that wouldn't be just about the numbers on the scoreboard. This one was about history—and about the man with a chance to make it.

Game 3: October 4, 2008

The Team You Couldn't Kill

MILWAUKEE—They were the team you just couldn't kill.

Every time you'd think those Milwaukee Brewers were heading for the town morgue, they'd keep springing back to life, like that pesky monster in *Alien*.

They'd seen those buildings crash around them for three weeks. They'd dodged more bullets than James Bond.

And now here they were again, still standing, still playing, still threatening to keep those Milwaukee crowds roaring and CC Sabathia wearing his Brewers shirt.

There they were, about to play Game 3 of the National League Division Series—down 0–2 in a series where three losses sends you home. That might sound like a major crisis for some teams, but for the Brewers, that just meant they had the Phillies right where they wanted them.

So *of course* the Brewers rose up to beat the Phillies, 4–1. *Of course* they got a win out of a pitcher (Dave Bush) who hadn't won since August 29—and hadn't beaten a team with a winning record since June 19.

Of course an offense that spent the first two games acting like a two-pitch at-bat was its idea of working the count forced Jamie Moyer to throw 62 pitches in the first two innings. *Of course* the Brew Crew got a save out of closer Salomon Torres after he'd loaded the bases with nobody out in the ninth.

Of course.

They wouldn't want it any other way. The bigger the mess, the happier they are.

"That's us," said Torres, after the Brewers had lived to play another day. "We're always fighting against the current—and always coming out on top."

When you've just found yourselves three games out in the loss column with a week left in the season—as the Brewers had—nobody needs to hand you a dictionary to spell out the meaning of that fabled term, "must-win game." They get the concept.

Must-win games are about the only kind this team had been playing since the middle of September. So what's another one? Or two? Or three? Been there. Done that. And now those Brewers were doing it again.

"We're tough, man," said center fielder Mike Cameron. "We've got ourselves a tough ballclub here."

And he ought to know. Nobody was the poster boy for "tough" like Cameron was in Game 3.

In between Game 2 and Game 3, not much happened in his life. Except that late-night team flight from Philadelphia to Milwaukee. And that arrival home about 2:00 AM. And then those "15 or 16 phone calls" from his wife at 4:30 AM to inform him that she'd just gone into labor—in Georgia.

And then a hectic scramble to the airport, another flight (to Atlanta), a race to the hospital to see his wife and his new daughter, Lilo. And then a few hours' sleep, yet one more sprint to one more airport, a

"Well," said one of the helpful media experts Counsell was conversing with, "apparently your manager did."

"That's his job, I guess," Counsell laughed. "That's why they give him that rule book, apparently."

Right. And Torres then reminded everybody why his team gives him the baseball by getting Carlos Ruiz to nub one back to the mound for the final out. And the Brewers were alive—for one more day.

Torres called this save "beautiful." But what it really was, was "perfect." One minute, it was a mess. The next minute, everything was fine. For one day, anyhow.

"Yeah, it was a mess," Counsell said. "And it's the messes we've been getting ourselves into.... But we've been doing a pretty good job getting out of those messes, too."

They weren't done getting out of this one, of course. They still needed to win Game 4, just to get a chance to get Sabathia back on the mound in Game 5. And the odds still weren't with them. They were well aware of that.

No National League team had ever fallen behind two games to zip in a best-of-five postseason series and come back to win it. But there's an asterisk to that stat, because the Brewers are one team that *had* done it.

That was the '82 Brewers, of course. And they played in the American League back then. But since this Brewers team spent all season celebrating that Brewers team (by wearing those '82 jerseys every Friday on Retro Night), this group knew all about that group. And it felt like just the kind of inspiration they needed.

"In the year 2025," said Hall, "we want somebody to wearing those '08 Brewers jerseys on Retro Night."

NL Division Series, Game 3,
October 4, 2008, at Milwaukee
Brewers 4, Phillies 1

Philadelphia	AB	R	H	RBI	BB	SO	LOB	AVG
Rollins, SS	4	0	1	0	0	1	1	.333
Werth, RF-LF	4	1	2	0	0	2	1	.333
Utley, 2B	4	0	1	0	0	0	1	.167
Howard, 1B	4	0	2	1	0	0	1	.250
Burrell, LF	3	0	0	0	0	0	2	.000
Eyre, P	0	0	0	0	0	0	0	.000
Madson, P	0	0	0	0	0	0	0	.000
b-Dobbs, PH	1	0	1	0	0	0	0	.500
Victorino, CF	4	0	1	0	0	0	2	.000
Feliz, 3B	4	0	1	0	0	0	4	.167
Ruiz, C	4	0	0	0	0	0	3	.100
Moyer, P	1	0	0	0	0	0	0	.000
a-Stairs, PH	1	0	0	0	0	0	1	.000
Condrey, P	0	0	0	0	0	0	0	.000
Durbin, C, P	0	0	0	0	0	0	0	.000
Jenkins, RF	1	0	0	0	0	0	0	.000
Totals	35	1	9	1	0	3	17	

Milwaukee	AB	R	H	RBI	BB	SO	LOB	AVG
Cameron, CF	2	2	1	0	2	0	2	.111
Hall, 3B	4	1	2	0	1	2	2	.286
Braun, LF	4	0	0	1	0	1	5	.250
Fielder, 1B	3	0	0	1	1	2	3	.000
Hardy, SS	4	1	3	1	0	0	2	.400
Hart, C, RF	2	0	1	0	1	1	1	.222
Weeks, 2B	1	0	0	0	0	0	0	.000
Counsell, 2B	3	0	1	0	0	1	3	.222
Kendall, C	4	0	2	1	0	0	0	.200
Bush, P	1	0	0	0	0	0	0	.000
Stetter, P	0	0	0	0	0	0	0	.000
Villanueva, P	1	0	1	0	0	0	0	1.000
a-Nelson, PH	1	0	0	0	0	1	2	.000
Gagne, P	0	0	0	0	0	0	0	.000
Torres, P	0	0	0	0	0	0	0	.000
Totals	30	4	11	4	5	8	20	

a-Flied out for Moyer in the 5th. b-Singled for Madson in the 9th.

BATTING
2B: Howard (1, Bush), Rollins (2, Bush), Werth (3, Gagne).
3B: Werth (1, Bush).
TB: Rollins 2; Werth 5; Utley; Howard 3; Dobbs; Victorino; Feliz.
RBI: Howard (1).
Runners left in scoring position, 2 out: Feliz; Werth; Victorino; Utley; Ruiz 2.
Team LOB: 7.

FIELDING
Outfield assists: Werth (Hart, C at 2nd base).

a-Struck out for Villanueva in the 7th.

BATTING
TB: Cameron; Hall 2; Hardy 3; Hart, C; Counsell; Kendall 2; Villanueva.
RBI: Fielder (1), Hardy (2), Braun (1), Kendall (1).
2-out RBI: Hardy.
Runners left in scoring position, 2 out: Hall; Counsell 2; Fielder 2; Cameron.
S: Bush; Hart, C.
SF: Fielder; Braun.
Team LOB: 12.

FIELDING
DP: (Hall-Counsell-Fielder).

Philadelphia	IP	H	R	ER	BB	SO	HR	ERA
Moyer (L, 0-1)	4.0	4	2	2	3	3	0	4.50
Condrey	1.0	1	1	1	2	1	0	9.00
Durbin, C	0.2	3	0	0	0	1	0	0.00
Eyre	1.0	3	1	1	0	0	0	9.00
Madson	1.1	0	0	0	0	2	0	0.00

Milwaukee	IP	H	R	ER	BB	SO	HR	ERA
Bush (W, 1-0)	5.1	5	1	1	0	3	0	1.69
Stetter (H, 1)	0.1	0	0	0	0	0	0	0.00
Villanueva (H, 1)	1.1	0	0	0	0	0	0	0.00
Gagne (H, 1)	1.0	1	0	0	0	0	0	0.00
Torres (S, 1)	1.0	3	0	0	0	0	0	0.00

WP: Moyer; IBB: Fielder (by Condrey); HBP: Cameron (by Condrey); Pitches-strikes: Moyer 90-55, Condrey 26-11, Durbin, C 20-13, Eyre 20-12, Madson 13-10, Bush 70-51, Stetter 5-3, Villanueva 16-12, Gagne 17-12, Torres 17-11; Groundouts-flyouts: Moyer 5-3, Condrey 0-2, Durbin, C 1-0, Eyre 1-1, Madson 1-1, Bush 4-9, Stetter 1-0, Villanueva 3-1, Gagne 1-2, Torres 2-0; Batters faced: Moyer 18, Condrey 7, Durbin, C 5, Eyre 6, Madson 4, Bush 21, Stetter 1, Villanueva 4, Gagne 4, Torres 5; Inherited runners-scored: Eyre 3-0, Madson 2-0, Stetter 1-1; Umpires: HP: Brian Runge. 1B: Fieldin Culbreth. 2B: Jim Joyce. 3B: Paul Nauert. LF: Dana DeMuth. RF: Mark Wegner.

Weather: 65 degrees, roof closed; Wind: 0 mph, None; T: 3:31; Att: 43,992.

Useless
Information

- At 45 years, 321 days old, Jamie Moyer became the oldest pitcher ever to lose a postseason game. The oldest before that: David Wells, who lost Game 2 of the 2006 NLDS at 43 years, 138 days old.

- Moyer didn't lose any of his final 10 regular-season starts (6–0, 3.55 ERA), but he lost the only game the Phillies would lose in this NLDS.

- Moyer did something in this game he'd done in just two of his 637 journeys to the mound in the regular season—he walked the first two hitters he faced. The only other times he'd done it: May 19, 1997 (Tony Phillips, Darin Erstad) and July 8, 1987 (Stan Jefferson, Tony Gwynn).

- For the third straight game, the Phillies scored all their runs in one inning—the third inning of Game 1, second inning of Game 2, and sixth inning of Game 3.

- Through three games of this series, the Phillies were batting a horrendous .161 (5-for-31) with runners in scoring position—and hadn't had a run-scoring hit since Shane Victorino's grand slam in the second inning of Game 2.

Game 4: October 5, 2008

So This Is
How It Feels

MILWAUKEE—No, Pat Burrell and Jimmy Rollins haven't been part of the Phillies for all of their 10,000 losses.

They weren't on the field when Mitch Williams gave up that home run to Joe Carter 15 Octobers ago. You can't blame them for any of those 10 games in a row the '64 Phillies lost in their ultimate tragic September.

So maybe Burrell and Rollins haven't quite seen it all since they arrived in America's most parade-starved city at the dawn of this millennium. But they've seen more than anybody around them, that's for sure. More losing. More angst. More stereophonic boo-fests. More everything.

But on the first Sunday of October, in a jam-packed dome in Milwaukee, the two longest-tenured Phillies on the roster got to witness something even they hadn't seen: The Phillies—their Phillies—winning an actual postseason series.

They closed out the Brewers in four games, whomping four homers, silencing 43,000 Thunderstix, and cruising to a 6–2 thumping that earned this team an NLCS appointment with the Dodgers.

But there was something fitting about the way this edition of a long-downtrodden franchise finished off the fifth postseason triumph in team history. This time, it was the two men who had worn this uniform the longest—Burrell and Rollins—who put the biggest stamp on the festivities.

Rollins sucked 2 billion decibels out of Miller Park with a stunning home run leading off the game. Burrell joined Leonard K. Dykstra on the list of Only Phillies in History to Hit Two Home Runs in One Postseason Game.

And afterward, no one had a greater appreciation for what all this meant than they did.

"It took a while to get here," said Burrell, the champagne waterfalling down his face. "But that just makes it all the sweeter now that you're here."

"I never wondered if this day would come," said Rollins, who hit .375 in this series. "I always knew it would."

How he knew is another story, though. It wasn't as if there was any positivity in the beginning to infuse him with that sort of hope. But there's no rational explanation for blind faith, and there doesn't really have to be.

Rollins joined the Phillies in September 2000, at the tail end of a 97-loss disaster. Burrell beat him to the big leagues by four months. Their first taste of big-league life was a gruesome march to nowhere, on a team that finished 30 games out of first place.

It was a taste neither of them could wait to expunge, like a giant plate of overcooked brussels sprouts.

"I always said, when I got here, that I wanted to try to change the tradition," Rollins said. "I said it to myself, *We need to change the mentality, change the way people think about this organization, change the way the young kids feel about being in this organization.* And the only way you can do that is by winning."

Well, it was still a little early to start lining up the parade floats. But they were getting there. At least this sure beat all those Septembers in their rearview mirror, when 6,000 people clattered around old Veterans Stadium and the only big games were visits by all those other teams, the ones that still had something to play for.

"To have played on some teams that were not very good," Burrell reminisced, "and to play against other teams in September that were getting ready to go on to the next level, I'll be honest. There was a sense of jealousy. You just wanted to be part of that, to experience that."

And now they have. Now they know. They've played in a half-dozen meaningful Septembers. They've felt the stab in their guts from a bunch of near-misses. They've sprayed champagne after two straight improbable NL East titles.

Then, after Game 4, they finally took the next step up that stairway to baseball heaven, by winning the first postseason series by a Phillies team in 15 years.

But they weren't just riding in the passenger seats, enjoying the October scenery. More than anyone in the ballpark, this was their show.

They've known each other since high school, these two native Northern Californians, since they played together in a California high school draft showcase called the Area Code Games. And they've been big-league teammates through more than 1,300 eventful baseball games.

So Rollins and Burrell know how to push each other's buttons when it matters most. And this was one of those times. After a Game 3 loss, with a potential Game 5 start by CC Sabathia lurking, this was a day to get it done. So suffice it to say the button-pushing was in full throttle.

"He was giving me some lip [in Game 3] about not getting [Ryan] Howard over," Burrell confessed after Game 4. "[Howard] was on second with no outs, and he's right, I didn't get him over. So I said, 'Hey, why don't *you* do something?'"

Joe Blanton follows through on a pitch during the sixth inning of Game 4 of the National League Division Series on October 5, 2008.

So, of course, Rollins did. He almost willed himself to do it, in fact.

The shortstop said he was thinking before the game, *You know what? It had been a long time since I hit a leadoff home run.* He said, "So I looked up at that blue sky and said, 'God, this would be a great time for it.'"

Bingo. On the sixth pitch of Game 4, Brewers starter Jeff Suppan served up a full-count meatball. Rollins lofted it into the right-field lower deck. And as he circled the bases, Burrell laughed to himself and said, "Okay, now it's on me."

Only a couple of hours earlier, in the early-morning dead time before a noon game, these two had had another conversation that turned out to be just as prescient.

"I walked in [to the clubhouse]," Rollins said. "And he said, 'They've been pitching around the big guy [Howard] and Chase [Utley].' And he said, 'I'm going to get 'em today.' He said, 'I feel good. My back's all right. I worked some things out in the cage.' He said it. I heard it. And I was paying attention."

Yep. Obviously. Too bad Brewers manager Dale Sveum wasn't.

With two outs in the third inning and that 1–0 Phillies lead still on the board, Sveum had a decision to make. Runner on third. Two outs. Howard heading for the plate. Burrell on deck.

It might seem like an easy call to hold up four fingers, whoosh Howard down to first base, and take on Burrell. But hang on for a second.

True, Howard had been just about the hottest hitter alive since September dawned. And Burrell had been just about the coldest. But not when Suppan was 60 feet away. Burrell had faced Suppan 28 times before that at-bat—and reached base in 16 of them (a .571 on-base percentage).

So as Burrell watched Howard trotting down the first-base line, he knew the Brewers had made the right decision. ("If I'm the manager, I'd do the same thing," Burrell admitted later. "You can't let Ryan Howard beat you.") But he also knew it was time to make them regret it.

Suppan floated a 2–2 fastball right down the chute. And Burrell smoked it off into the distance, directly into the middle of an unsuspecting nacho plate on the deck of Friday's Front Row Sports Grill, for a 4–0 Phillies lead.

"It was kinda like, 'Drop the beer, keep the nachos,' right there," Rollins chuckled later, in a clubhouse full of people who were a lot happier than those diners.

And once Burrell had finished trotting around the diamond, this series was never the same again. Three pitches later, Jayson Werth cranked the Phillies' third homer of the day. And five innings after that, Burrell would foil another Sveum brainstorm—yanking Manny Parra and bringing on right-hander Guillermo Mota, just for him—with his second home run of the day.

It made Burrell only the fifth National Leaguer in history to hit two home runs in a series-clinching game. You've probably heard of the others: Steve Garvey (1974 NLCS), Johnny Bench (1976 World Series), Fred McGriff (1995 NLDS), and Carlos Beltran (2004 NLDS).

But it also made him something much more important—a man who had finally made a meaningful contribution to a team making its first real October run in a generation.

Before this game, Burrell's lifetime postseason batting average was worse than Brett Myers'—as in .105 (2-for-19). And even worse, he'd gone 0-for-this-series as the Phillies scuffled for offense.

So this wasn't just a game for the memory banks. This was a game that pumped oxygen back into the lungs of a guy who wanted desperately to leave an imprint on the only franchise he has ever played for.

"In April or something, if you had three games where you didn't get any hits and really weren't a factor, it doesn't seem to be as magnified," Burrell said. "But when you get into a situation like this, where the emotions are there, and all the excitement, and you care, to not be a factor

Jimmy Rollins hits a home run during the first inning of Game 4 of the
National League Division Series on October 5, 2008.

and not help your team win—it gets old. It affects you. So I was just happy to be a factor and contribute. That's all it was."

He was 21 years old a decade ago, when the Phillies made him the first player picked in the country in the June '98 draft. Now it was half a lifetime later. He was days away from turning 32. And with free agency looming, these would be his final days as a Phillie.

But that's a topic for another time. This was about floating inside a moment he'd waited his career for—and fulfilling the 2008 vision of his old friend, Jimmy Rollins.

Way back in the cold of winter, Rollins raised the bar for the 2008 edition of his franchise by predicting his team would win 100 games. Now, here they were at 95 and still playing. And Rollins never did say the Phillies would win those 100 games during the regular season, now, did he?

"You know, that's what's great about [those predictions]," Rollins deadpanned. "You can always adjust."

So does this, someone asked, mean the Phillies are the team to beat?

"Hey," smiled the great oracle of Philadelphia. "Now we'll find out. Won't we?"

NL Division Series, Game 4,
October 5, 2008, at Milwaukee
Phillies 6, Brewers 2

Philadelphia	AB	R	H	RBI	BB	SO	LOB	AVG
Rollins, SS	4	1	2	1	0	0	0	.375
Victorino, CF	4	1	1	0	0	0	1	.357
Utley, 2B	3	0	0	0	1	1	1	.133
Howard, 1B	3	1	0	0	1	1	1	.182
Burrell, LF	4	2	3	4	0	0	0	.250
Bruntlett, LF	0	0	0	0	0	0	0	1.000
Werth, RF	4	1	1	1	0	1	1	.313
Dobbs, 3B	3	0	2	0	0	0	0	.600
Feliz, 3B	1	0	1	0	0	0	0	.231
Ruiz, C	4	0	0	0	0	1	4	.071
Blanton, P	3	0	0	0	0	3	2	.000
Madson, P	0	0	0	0	0	0	0	.000
a-Stairs, PH	1	0	0	0	0	0	1	.000
Lidge, P	0	0	0	0	0	0	0	.000
Totals	34	6	10	6	2	7	11	

a-Grounded into a double play for Madson in the 9th.

Milwaukee	AB	R	H	RBI	BB	SO	LOB	AVG
Cameron, CF	4	1	1	0	0	1	1	.154
Durham, 2B	4	0	0	0	0	1	2	.125
Braun, LF	4	0	2	1	0	2	1	.313
Fielder, 1B	4	1	1	1	0	0	2	.071
Hardy, SS	4	0	2	0	0	0	0	.429
Hart, C, RF	4	0	1	0	0	1	2	.231
Counsell, 3B	3	0	0	0	0	1	2	.167
Mota, P	0	0	0	0	0	0	0	.000
c-Nelson, PH	1	0	0	0	0	1	1	.000
Kendall, C	4	0	0	0	0	0	3	.143
Suppan, P	0	0	0	0	0	0	0	.000
a-Sabathia, PH	1	0	0	0	0	1	0	.000
Gallardo, P	0	0	0	0	0	0	0	.000
b-Gwynn, PH	1	0	1	0	0	0	0	.333
Parra, P	0	0	0	0	0	0	0	.000
Hall, 3B	1	0	0	0	0	0	0	.250
Totals	35	2	8	2	0	8	14	

a-Struck out for Suppan in the 3rd. b-Singled for Gallardo in the 6th. c-Struck out for Mota in the 9th.

BATTING
2B: Victorino (3, Suppan).
HR: Rollins (1, 1st inning off Suppan, 0 on, 0 out). Burrell 2 (2, 3rd inning off Suppan, 2 on, 2 out; 8th inning off Mota, 0 on, 2 out), Werth (1, 3rd inning off Suppan, 0 on, 2 out).
TB: Rollins 5; Victorino 2; Burrell 9; Werth 4; Dobbs 2; Feliz.
RBI: Rollins (1), Burrell 4 (4), Werth (1).
2-out RBI: Burrell 4; Werth.
Runners left in scoring position, 2 out: Blanton 2.
GIDP: Howard; Victorino; Stairs.
Team LOB: 3.

BATTING
HR: Fielder (1, 7th inning off Blanton, 0 on, 0 out).
TB: Cameron; Braun 2; Fielder 4; Hardy 2; Hart; C; Gwynn.
RBI: Fielder (2), Braun (2).
2-out RBI: Braun.
Runners left in scoring position, 2 out: Kendall 2.
Team LOB: 6.

FIELDING
DP: 3 (Counsell-Hardy-Fielder, Hardy-Durham-Fielder, Hardy-Fielder).

Philadelphia	IP	H	R	ER	BB	SO	HR	ERA
Blanton (W, 1-0)	6.0	5	1	1	0	7	1	1.50
Madson	2.0	2	1	1	0	0	0	2.25
Lidge	1.0	1	0	0	0	1	0	3.00

Milwaukee	IP	H	R	ER	BB	SO	HR	ERA
Suppan (L, 0-1)	3.0	6	5	5	2	3	3	15.00
Gallardo	3.0	1	0	0	0	1	0	0.00
Parra	1.2	1	0	0	0	3	0	0.00
Mota	1.1	2	1	1	0	0	1	5.40

Blanton pitched to 2 batters in the 7th.

WP: Suppan; IBB: Howard (by Suppan); Pitches-strikes: Blanton 107-72, Madson 25-18, Lidge 16-10, Suppan 65-41, Gallardo 36-26, Parra 18-11, Mota 16-12; Groundouts-flyouts: Blanton 2-9, Madson 4-2, Lidge 2-0, Suppan 3-3, Gallardo 4-4, Parra 2-0, Mota 3-1; Batters faced: Blanton 23, Madson 8, Lidge 4, Suppan 16, Gallardo 10, Parra 5, Mota 5; Inherited runners-scored: Madson 1-0; Umpires: HP: Fielin Culbreth. 1B: Jim Joyce. 2B: Paul Nauert. 3B: Dana DeMuth. LF: Mark Wegner. RF: Brian Runge.

Weather: 66 degrees, roof closed; Wind: 0 mph, None; T: 2:53; Att: 43,934.

Useless
Information

- Joe Blanton became the second Phillies starter not named Steve Carlton to win the clincher of a postseason series. The other: Tommy Greene, in the 1993 NLCS.

- Before Blanton, only three pitchers in history had changed teams in midseason and won a postseason clincher. The others, according to the Elias Sports Bureau: Jeff Weaver (2006 Cardinals), David Wells (1995 Reds), and Mike Torrez (1977 Yankees).

- This was the Phillies' first four-homer postseason game in team history. And it *still* didn't feel like a shocker. Their lineup owned nine career homers in 99 at-bats against Milwaukee's Game 4 starter, Jeff Suppan.

- Jimmy Rollins led off Game 4 with a home run. He'd kicked off only one road game all season with a leadoff homer—way back on April 7, in Game 6 of the season.

- Only one Phillie had ever driven in more runs in a postseason game than the four Pat Burrell knocked in—his hitting coach (Milt Thompson, in Game 4 of the 1993 World Series).

We know now how this turned out. We know now that the Dodgers weren't the hottest, most dangerous team in the October field. We know now it was actually the Phillies who were even hotter, even more dangerous. But we didn't know that in the first week of October. Did we?

The Dodgers team that rolled into Philadelphia to start the National League Championship Series had just swept the Cubs, the team with the best record in the league. The Dodgers team that rolled into Philadelphia had gone 22–8 since August 30. And the Dodgers team that rolled into Philadelphia employed a fellow named Manny Ramirez, who had just finished hitting .396, with 17 homers, a .469 on-base percentage, and a .743 slugging percentage in his two months as a Dodger—a set of numbers unmatched by any midseason acquisition in the history of baseball.

Well, the Phillies never would control Manny—in more ways than one. But stuff kept on happening—the kind of stuff that never used to happen to other Phillies teams that tried to navigate the October mine fields. What kind of stuff? Read on. It's all right here, in Part 4 of this opus.

What's That Sound? History-Makers at Work

PHILADELPHIA—It was just another autumn Tuesday. But passersby reported a strange sound at the corner of Darien Street and Pattison Avenue in South Philadelphia. It was odd, all right. It sounded almost like, well, baseball. In a month that most of us know as October. How 'bout that?

As it turned out, it was just the sound of the Phillies tuning up for their National League Championship Series with the Dodgers. But you could understand why that's a sound that could scare off many an unsuspecting pedestrian.

In case you hadn't studied up on this sort of thing, you see, not many people in Philadelphia are familiar with the concept that baseball can still be played in October.

The leaves turn in October. Pumpkins get carved in October. The Eagles throw those shoulder pads on in October. But the Phillies? For 95 of the last 106 Octobers (a.k.a., the World Series era), they've been officially invisible by October, unless they had a manager to fire or something.

So for the current group of Phillies, there was more going on here than just another baseball team trying to reach for another October mountaintop. This was a group on a mission—a mission to rewrite history. Its own.

It's very rare in sports that you hear players talk about this sort of thing. But it happened in the first week in October, in a clubhouse celebrating only the fifth victory in any postseason series in franchise history.

"I always said, when I got here, that I wanted to try to change the tradition," said Jimmy Rollins, a man who actually thinks these concepts through—and verbalizes them, right out loud, in front of real witnesses. "I said it to myself, 'We need to change the mentality, change the way people think about this organization, change the way the young kids feel about being in this organization.' And the only way you can do that is by winning."

So Rollins and the core group of this team have constantly raised the bar. A little higher. Then a little higher than that. Then a little higher than that. Until it brought them to this time and place—where they had an opportunity to carve a new chapter all their own. A chapter they might even enjoy reading some day.

And there haven't been a whole lot of enjoyable chapters like that in the life of this franchise, you understand. Need a brief history lesson? Here goes:

You might be shocked to learn that before the Cubs forgot to win the World Series for a century, the Phillies were the team whose record they broke. It took the Phillies 98 seasons to win their first World Series, in 1980. And, as you might have noticed, they hadn't won one since. Heck, even the Royals had won a World Series more recently than the Phillies.

Part 4
The National League Championship Series

But it hasn't just been the World Series that Phillies teams have had a little trouble with. It's been every kind of postseason series.

The Marlins have been around for 16 seasons. They've won six postseason series. The Phillies have been in existence for slightly longer than that—like by 110 years. But as the NLCS dawned, they'd only won *five* postseason series in the history of the franchise.

"You know, I was watching ESPN the day we beat the Brewers, and I saw that," said catcher Chris Coste. "They said it was only the fifth postseason victory here. That stunned me. It really did. I don't know how many of us knew that."

In this case, though, ignorance is bliss. The less these players knew about the 125 seasons before this one, the better off they'd be. Fortunately, when we took a quick survey of the clubhouse to determine how much these men knew about their franchise before they arrived, they confessed to a dazzling array of historical obliviousness.

"To be honest," said Chase Utley, when we posed that question, "I knew very little."

So what would constitute "very little," we asked.

"Uh, zero?" he laughed.

Then there was third baseman Greg Dobbs. He "had no idea" about what went on in Philadelphia all those years before he checked in last year. "I had none," Dobbs said. "I really didn't. Not one iota.

"I mean, I knew about Steve Carlton," Dobbs offered, just so he wouldn't flunk this test too disastrously. "I knew Jack Schmidt—I mean Michael Jack Schmidt. I knew those names. I knew [Bob] Boone. But being a West Coast guy, playing in Seattle all those years, I had no clue what I was walking into."

Fortunately, though, these fellows have had the always-helpful fans of Philadelphia to turn to. And those fans have been working overtime to fill in the blanks—just to make sure these guys were all caught up on important historical tidbits like the collapse of the '64 Phillies, the Black Friday debacle of October 1977, and, well, just about every other dark day in Phillies history.

"When we had that 10,000ᵗʰ loss [in franchise history] last year, I don't think one player in here knew about that up until we approached it," said Coste. "But once we got to that 10,000ᵗʰ loss, the fans let us know about it—as if *we* lost all 10,000 games."

The Red Sox, by the way, could lose every game they play between now and the year 2020 and *still* not have 10,000 losses. And while we're on the subject, the Phillies could also win the next three World Series in succession and still not have as many A) championships or B) postseason series won as the Red Sox.

But for some reason, the Phillies have never gotten their due in this great country we live in as a preeminent semitragic franchise. There are trillions of Americans who can run through every lost October opportunity in the life of the Red Sox and Cubs. But the Phillies' 125 years of futility? Only the people in the cheese-steak line at Pat's Steaks seem to be totally up on that one.

"I think Fenway has a lot to do with it," said Mitch Williams, the remarkably beloved closer on the last Phillies team to win a postseason series (and last to lose a World Series), the 1993 juggernaut. "Fenway is kind of a national landmark. And so is Wrigley. The field has never changed. So everyone wants to go to Fenway. Everyone wants to go to Wrigley. No one wanted to come to the Vet [i.e., the late, great Veterans Stadium]. I mean, all they ever heard about the Vet is, they had rats in there that could carry a man off."

So apparently, giant rats don't carry the same kind of poetic weight as ivy? Who knew?

But there were, of course, some good things that happened at old Vet Stadium, too. The 1976–1977–1978 Phillies won three NL East titles in a row there (and made three straight first-round postseason exits). And the 1980 Phillies carved the happiest memories in Phillies history there.

By 2008, though, the Vet had been defunct for five seasons. And a new generation of Phillies looked at its new ballpark as a blank canvas where this group could create a whole different kind of masterpiece—starting right here.

"I think step one, phase one, was getting out of the Vet," said Rollins, "and getting to somewhere where you could kind of erase the history of all the wrongdoings that happened there and only winning one World Series. The 1980 squad, that [was] their home. No matter who you were or what you did, you were always playing where Mike Schmidt and the 1980 squad won the World Series.

"So I told Larry Bowa [before the Vet got imploded], that was the house that he had built, and across the street is going to be the house that *we* build. And this is a step in the right direction."

Whether this team was ready to take the last two steps in that direction, all the way to the parade floats, we wouldn't know for three more weeks. But this was a group that seemed atypically aware of the opportunity it had—at this moment in time—to leave its imprint on the mostly dark history of the franchise.

"When you look back, the Philadelphia Phillies have been around for a long time," Dobbs said. "So there is a certain legacy. And you hope that you can leave an imprint on that legacy in the time that you were with that organization, that you were able to accomplish something special for the organization, for the city, for the town, and for your teammates. So I would have to agree with Jimmy.... You do want to leave your stamp on this era, because as soon as it comes, it can be gone as well.

"There has been so much made here of the losses and the failures," Dobbs went on. "Which I understand. There are always two sides to it. There are the wins and the losses. You have to take the good with the bad. But to be able to maybe put that to rest once and for all, and maybe have the sun shine a little bit more on the organization when people look at it from the outside.... I think we all, deep down, want that."

Manny Ramirez and his buddies would have other ideas, obviously. But if the calendar said it was October and the Phillies were still playing baseball, then that meant their history was still in their hands. And if they didn't rewrite it, at least it wouldn't be because they didn't understand the urgency of the moment.

"It's crunch time," Dobbs said. "Big lights. Big city. We're playing the best of the best. It doesn't get any more urgent than that."

Game 1: October 9, 2008

Citizens Arrest

PHILADELPHIA—Not even submarines sink like a Derek Lowe sinkerball.

It's more than a pitch. It's a subterranean robot.

And for five innings in Game 1 of the National League Championship Series, that Derek Lowe sinkerball was doing exactly what it's designed to do to offenses like the Phillies'—squishing defenseless blades of grass all over the infield at Citizens Bank Park.

So as the bottom of the sixth arrived, not even the Psychic Hotline could have predicted the turn of events that was about to lead the Phillies to an improbable 3–2 win over Lowe and the Dodgers.

One minute, the Phillies didn't look like a team that could get a ball airborne with a tennis racket. The next, two stunning home runs were floating through the electrified October night, those rally towels were swirling, and the look on Derek Lowe's face said it all.

Loosely translated, you could describe that look this way: "This frigging park is a joke."

He'd just watched a game-tying, two-run, Chase Utley home run come down in the third row of the right-field lower deck. He'd just watched what turned out to be a game-winning homer by Pat Burrell return to earth in the second row of the left-field lower deck.

And nobody had to get out a site map to explain to Derek Lowe—or anyone in a Dodgers uniform—that had they all been playing baseball in L.A. instead of Philadelphia, those mighty blows would *not* have been home runs on anybody's scorecard.

But as that noted wise man, Manny Ramirez, observed sagely afterward, "We're not in L.A."

Right he was, of course. And it would also be 100 percent right to mention that this wasn't exactly the first time crazy things had happened to pitchers like Derek Lowe in the Phillies' cozy little home park. But maybe not *this* crazy. After all, consider the big picture here:

- Heading into the sixth, 11 of Lowe's 13 non-strikeout outs had been ground-ball outs—and the only member of the Phillies' lineup who had made an out in the air was leadoff man Jimmy Rollins, who had made two of them (pop-up to first, fly ball to left).

- Also heading into the sixth, Lowe had given up two home runs to the previous 286 hitters he'd faced—a span that included 12 starts over the last eight weeks.

- And the two guys who were about to homer off him, Utley and Burrell, had faced him a combined 44 times in their respective careers—and never hit *any* homers.

But in October, past history often seems about as relevant to current events as the French-Indian War. So an hour later, Derek Lowe found himself standing at his locker, talking about his first loss to the Phillies since 2001 and doing his best not to blame the ballpark, its architects, or anyone else responsible for this loss—except himself.

"It's a hitter's park, but that doesn't mean you can't pitch a good game," said Lowe, the man who, until those home runs, had been the hottest starting pitcher still standing in this postseason (7–1, 1.41 ERA in his previous 11 starts). "You know, hindsight in this game will make you not sleep at night. You're thinking, *Why did I throw that pitch? Why didn't I try something else?*

"This," said Derek Lowe, "was a what-if game."

Okay, so let's ask that question right along with him.

What if his shortstop, Rafael Furcal, hadn't tried to rush his throw to first on the Shane Victorino chopper that started the fateful bottom of the sixth?

Furcal would later say the ball had just "slipped out of my hand." And Lowe would later absolve his shortstop of all culpability. But Phillies manager Charlie Manuel had a different view.

"I thought maybe when Furcal threw the ball away at first base," Manuel said, "I felt like that was kind of a turn for us."

And what if, on the other hand, Ramirez's 409-foot laser beam to center field in the first inning had been hit just a few feet higher—and clanked off, say, the flagpole for a two-run homer instead of clattering off the grate above the *409* sign for an RBI double?

"You know what? I've never seen a ball hit that fence," Victorino said. "In the three, four years I've been here, I have never, ever seen that. Usually, when a ball gets hit out there, either it goes up into the seats or it hits the wall and kicks off funny and the center fielder is doing a dance trying to chase it down. But I've never seen that."

Well, whatever happened, Ramirez wound up getting stranded at third base. And the Dodgers did, after all, lose by just one run.

But the biggest *what if* of all is what would have happened if this game had merely been played 3,000 miles to the west? We'll never know the answer to that one, though. And Derek Lowe didn't even want to know.

Los Angeles Dodgers manager Joe Torre shakes hands with Charlie Manuel before Game 1 of the National League Championship Series on October 9, 2008.

All he knew was that one pitch after the Furcal error, he laid a first-pitch fastball in there to Utley, waist-high. And even though Utley was clearly bothered by a much-rumored hip injury and hit just .133 in the NLDS, he was a man with a plan on this pitch.

"I know better than that," Lowe bludgeoned himself. "They had just gotten a guy to second base. And the crowd was into it. And I pretty much knew he was going to swing at the first pitch. And I should know better. I left a ball out over the plate and, well, there you go."

Yeah, there it went, all right. And Lowe's hard-earned 2–0 lead had officially disappeared. Then, nine pitches after that, Lowe elevated another sinker on a 3-and-1 count. Burrell pummeled it into the towel rack in left. And this game had U-turned—for good.

"Same [mistake] with Burrell's ball," Lowe muttered. "It's 3-and-1. And in this park, walks will kill you. So it was the same kind of pitch. Just left it out over the plate and...."

And *kaboom*. In what seemed like about 45 seconds, he'd gone from being in total control of what was shaping up to be his fifth consecutive postseason win (dating back to the 2004 Red Sox) to a disaster he'd never seen coming.

Then along came Joe Torre, stalking toward the mound. And Chan Ho Park was trotting out of the bullpen. And the 45,839 occupants of his favorite ballpark were working on a serious case of mass laryngitis. Whew. How had it all changed on him so fast?

"Things happen quick in this game of baseball," said Victorino. "A lot of times, in any sport, momentum shifts sometimes off a simple mistake, or a big home run, or a big pitch. In this case, that Furcal error just swayed it a little bit our way. And then Chase came up with the big home run. And you could feel it in the air."

But what exactly were they feeling? On one hand, this game still exposed the Phillies' biggest areas of vulnerabilities. They scored just three runs, they scored in only one inning (for the fourth time in five postseason games), and they scored only via the home run (which had

Pat Burrell hits a home run off the Dodgers' Derek Lowe (23) during sixth inning of Game 1 of the National League Championship Series on October 9, 2008.

accounted for 12 of their 18 October runs so far). But they didn't seem too devastated by any of that.

"A win is a win is a win," laughed hitting coach Milt Thompson. "The object is to score more runs than the other team."

On the other hand, the Phillies did find a way to beat a pitcher who was 5–0 with a 0.85 ERA against them in his previous seven starts. And their heretofore missing-in-action middle of the order generated all three runs (after hitting a combined .184 in the LDS). And above all, the Phillies again did what they'd been doing best for four weeks now—finding some way, somehow, to scramble from behind and win.

"I've seen this so many times," said closer Brad Lidge, who spun off a 1-2-3 ninth in his first NLCS appearance since the Albert Pujols Game. "We can be down five or six runs, and mentally, I'm thinking what do I have to do to get ready [for a save opportunity] when we come back and take the lead, because we've done it so many times."

They seemed like the underdog in this series. Yet they were now 4–1 in this postseason, and 17–4 in their last 21 games. And you know that August 30 date when the Dodgers turned on the jets to go 22–9? The Phillies actually had an even better record since then (23–9).

And the really terrifying thing for the rest of the October field is: The more they rose up to win games like this, the more dangerous they looked.

"Confidence," said Jimmy Rollins. "It's confidence. We all look for the big moment. There's no doubt about that. We're not afraid of it. We all want to join the party."

Well, the party was raging in South Philadelphia on this night, all thanks to a couple of hanging sinkers and a ballpark where hanging sinkers go to die. But somehow, this felt like more than that—even to the losing pitcher.

"That," said Derek Lowe, "is a real good team over there."

NL Championship Series, Game 1, October 9, 2008, at Philadelphia
Phillies 3, Dodgers 2

LA Dodgers	AB	R	H	RBI	BB	SO	LOB	AVG
Furcal, SS	4	0	0	0	0	0	0	.000
Ethier, RF	4	1	2	0	0	2	0	.500
Ramirez, M, LF	4	0	2	1	0	0	1	.500
Martin, C	3	0	1	0	1	2	2	.333
Loney, 1B	3	0	1	0	1	1	3	.333
Kemp, CF	4	1	1	0	0	0	3	.250
Blake, 3B	4	0	0	0	0	1	1	.000
DeWitt, 2B	3	0	0	1	0	2	0	.000
Lowe, P	2	0	0	0	0	1	0	.000
Park, P	0	0	0	0	0	0	0	.000
a-Kent, PH	1	0	0	0	0	1	0	.000
Maddux, P	0	0	0	0	0	0	0	.000
Kuo, P	0	0	0	0	0	0	0	.000
Totals	32	2	7	2	2	10	10	

a-Struck out for Park in the 7th.

BATTING
2B: Ethier (1, Hamels), Ramirez, M (1, Hamels), Kemp (1, Hamels).
TB: Ethier 3; Ramirez, M 3; Martin; Loney; Kemp 2.
RBI: Ramirez, M (1), DeWitt (1).
Runners left in scoring position, 2 out: Kemp 2; Loney.
SF: DeWitt.
GIDP: Kemp.
Team LOB: 6.

FIELDING
E: Furcal (1, throw).
DP: 2 (DeWitt-Loney 2).

Philadelphia	AB	R	H	RBI	BB	SO	LOB	AVG
Rollins, SS	4	0	0	0	0	0	3	.000
Victorino, CF	4	1	0	0	0	0	0	.000
Utley, 2B	4	1	2	2	0	1	0	.500
Howard, 1B	4	0	0	0	0	0	1	.000
Burrell, LF	3	1	2	1	0	1	0	.667
Lidge, P	0	0	0	0	0	0	0	.000
Werth, RF	3	0	0	0	0	0	1	.000
Feliz, 3B	2	0	0	0	1	0	0	.000
Ruiz, C	3	0	2	0	0	0	1	.667
Hamels, P	2	0	1	0	0	0	0	.500
a-Taguchi, PH	1	0	0	0	0	0	1	.000
Madson, P	0	0	0	0	0	0	0	.000
Bruntlett, LF	0	0	0	0	0	0	0	.000
Totals	30	3	7	3	1	2	7	

a-Bunted out for Hamels in the 7th.

BATTING
HR: Utley (1, 6th inning off Lowe, 1 on, 0 out), Burrell (1, 6th inning off Lowe, 0 on, 1 out).
TB: Utley 5; Burrell 5; Ruiz 2; Hamels.
RBI: Utley 2 (2), Burrell (1).
Runners left in scoring position, 2 out: Rollins.
GIDP: Werth; Rollins.
Team LOB: 4.

FIELDING
PB: Ruiz (1).
DP: (Rollins-Utley-Howard).

LA Dodgers	IP	H	R	ER	BB	SO	HR	ERA
Lowe (L, 0-1)	5.1	6	3	2	1	2	2	3.38
Park	0.2	0	0	0	0	0	0	0.00
Maddux	1.0	1	0	0	0	0	0	0.00
Kuo	1.0	0	0	0	0	0	0	0.00

Philadelphia	IP	H	R	ER	BB	SO	HR	ERA
Hamels (W, 1-0)	7.0	6	2	2	2	8	0	2.57
Madson (H, 1)	1.0	1	0	0	0	1	0	0.00
Lidge (S, 1)	1.0	0	0	0	0	1	0	0.00

Pitches-strikes: Lowe 90-55, Park 8-5, Maddux 8-5, Kuo 10-5, Hamels 105-70, Madson 10-7, Lidge 13-9; Groundouts-flyouts: Lowe 12-2, Park 1-1, Maddux 2-1, Kuo 1-2, Hamels 9-4, Madson 1-1, Lidge 0-2; Batters faced: Lowe 23, Park 2, Maddux 3, Kuo 3, Hamels 28, Madson 4, Lidge 3; Umpires: HP: Mike Reilly. 1B: Jerry Meals. 2B: Mike Everitt. 3B: Ted Barrett. LF: Mike Winters. RF: Gary Cederstrom.

Weather: 73 degrees, partly cloudy; Wind: 8 mph, Out to RF; T: 2:36; Att: 45,839.

Useless
Information

- Jimmy Rollins, Shane Victorino, and Ryan Howard all went 0-for-4 in Game 1—and the Phillies still found a way to win. So how many previous times had the Phillies won a game in which all three of those guys went hitless in at least four at-bats? That would be *none*, of course—in their entire career together.

- Chase Utley and Pat Burrell both homered off Derek Lowe in the sixth inning. Before that, Lowe had allowed exactly *one* two-homer inning in his previous 40 regular-season and postseason starts.

- Cole Hamels faced 27 hitters in his NLDS start against the Brewers and gave up a hit to two of them. So, naturally, he allowed a hit to two of the first three hitters he faced in this game.

- This was the Phillies' fourth win of the postseason, and in three of them they scored all their runs in one inning. According to the Elias Sports Bureau, they were just the third team in history to win three games like that in one postseason. The others: Charlie Hayes' 1996 Yankees and George Herman Ruth's 1918 Red Sox.

- Utley's homer off Lowe came on the first pitch. Utley hadn't hit a first-pitch homer against anyone since April 23.

Life and Game 2 Collide

PHILADELPHIA—A baseball is round. A circle is round. But as Charlie Manuel proved on this bittersweet day, it isn't always easy for that baseball to fit inside the circle of life.

Charlie Manuel has managed 1,080 games in the big leagues, but he's never managed a game quite like Game 2 of the National League Championship Series.

It was one of the most satisfying games of his managerial career. It was also the saddest. It was the day his Phillies fought to within two games of the World Series with a raucous 8–5 win over the Dodgers, a win that gave them a 2-games-to-0 lead in the NLCS. But that was just the part of this day that revolved around baseball.

It was Charlie Manuel's other journey, his journey along that circle of life, that made a mere postseason baseball game feel almost insignificant.

It was the day the manager came to the ballpark knowing that this was one day that wouldn't end with the favorite postgame ritual of his managerial life—that daily phone call from June Manuel, the mother who raised him, loved him, and affectionately picked apart every game he ever managed.

June Manuel was rushed to a Virginia hospital three days before this game. She passed away just hours before it began. So for the better part of the week, the manager had been a jumble of swirling emotions. How could he not be?

Yet he told almost no one around him. In the most important week of his managerial career, he made one of life's most difficult choices.

He didn't merely decide to stay with his team. He decided to do everything he could to make sure the *story* of the week was his team.

"I had no idea what he was going through until today," said Phillies third baseman Greg Dobbs, after his team's sixth win in seven postseason games. "But that's Charlie. He didn't want to burden this team with what he was going through personally. He's done a very good job of masking his thoughts around us."

But on this day, that was no longer possible. His first-base coach, Davey Lopes, floated through the clubhouse before Game 2, letting players know why their manager might not be his usual garrulous self.

His players, in turn, let the manager know this would be no ordinary day for them, either. This one wasn't for themselves. It was for June Manuel and the son who has helped bond this group into one of the closest teams in sports.

"I told him right before we went out there, 'I'm going to win this one for your mom,'" said the starting pitcher, Brett Myers.

And even as this game rolled along, enveloping Myers in a bunch of wild and wacky plotlines—a three-hit day at the plate, a mildly sprained ankle on one of his two harrowing trips around the bases, an 8–2 lead almost returned to sender—the man on the mound couldn't get the man in the dugout out of his mind.

"I even told him after the third inning," Myers said. "I went up and gave him a hug and said, 'I love you, man,' because I was thinking about his mom. I was thinking about what a good person he is for this team."

That would have been a powerful moment had it been anyone on the roster. But it was especially meaningful that this was Brett Myers going out of his way to envelop his manager with compassion.

It was only a couple of months earlier, you may recall, that Myers and Manuel had a public shouting match, right there in this very dugout, with the TV cameras rolling and thousands of witnesses watching it all unfold.

If that had been another manager, their YouTube moment might have built an impenetrable wall between them, even spiraled into a one-of-these-men-must-go soap opera. But Charlie Manuel has a way of rising above that sort of pettiness.

He's a man with an innate understanding of the emotions that drive baseball players to the pinnacle of irrationality—and a man with the ability to distinguish what matters from what doesn't.

"Charlie's a guy who's always there for you," Myers said. "That's what he does. He's not a different guy the next day if you pitch bad. He's still there for you.

"I think we know each other's personalities. And I think that's one thing that he has in his corner. He knows everybody's personality in here. He knows how to handle every one of us. And that's what makes him so good with me, because he knows that if I blow up at something, it's just because I was in the moment and I'm a competitor. He knows all that. And that's why it was so easy to get over whatever spat we had."

If this had been a normal day at the ballpark—assuming there's any such thing in October—it would have been Myers, not his manager, who was the No. 1 topic of conversation. In the annals of madcap days by starting pitchers in postseason history, Myers' day has to rank right near the top of the list.

Shane Victorino watches his two-run scoring single against pitcher Chad Billingsley during Game 2 of the National League Championship Series on October 10, 2008.

He planted one first-inning fastball under Manny Ramirez's armpits. He launched another 94-mile-an-hour smokeball behind Ramirez's dreadlocks. Then, on the heels of his mind-warping 19-pitches-in-two-duels-with–CC Sabathia day at the plate in the NLDS, Myers followed up that act by becoming the first pitcher since 1919 to have a three-hit, three-RBI game on any grand October stage.

Just for perspective's sake, we're talking about a fellow who hadn't previously been confused with Ty Cobb. Myers went a spectacular 4-for-58 at the plate this season, with one RBI. So now here he was in October, 4-for-5 with three RBIs. What the heck was up with that, anyhow?

Okay, here's what: Afterward, his hitting coach, Milt Thompson, made the mistake of mentioning that Myers has spread out at the plate like (gasp) Albert Pujols. "Look, he'll never *be* Albert Pujols," Thompson said. "But he's put himself in better position up there."

Naturally, it didn't take long for word to reach Myers that his hitting coach had just dropped his name and Pujols' name in the same sentence. Myers nodded approvingly, as if he were shocked that it took this long for the world to catch on to their many similarities.

"That's 100 percent right," Myers deadpanned. "I'm a deep threat, you know. I can bloop one over second base."

"You think Albert has patterned himself after you?" someone asked.

"If anyone patterns themselves after the way I hit," Myers retorted, "they need to just not play anymore."

So stay tuned for Pujols' imminent retirement announcement any minute now. But in the meantime, once Myers had finished making two zany treks around the bases and the Phillies had finished reeling off consecutive four-run innings, this was an 8–2 game after only three innings. And Citizens Bank Park was reverberating with breathless chants of "Beat L.A."

But just minutes later, it was reverberating from a different sort of shock wave—the shock of seeing Ramirez mash a three-run home run into the petunia garden in left, turning a blowout into an 8–5 this-is-life-in-Philly special.

And that brings us to the other character in this circle-of-life production—center fielder Shane Victorino.

Victorino played this game not knowing that tragedy had also interjected itself into his life. On a day when his 82-year-old grandmother, Irene Victorino, had died earlier in the day, Victorino singled in two runs in the second inning, tripled in two more in the third, and then hauled out his most special moment of the day when his team needed it most.

With two outs in the seventh and the tying run at the plate, Victorino splattered himself against the wall in deep left-center to rob Casey Blake of at least a double, keep at least two runs off the board, and save millions of Philadelphians from stampeding straight to their favorite cardiologists. "A game-changing catch," teammate Jayson Werth called it.

It was only later, after Brad Lidge had whiffed Matt Kemp and Nomar Garciaparra with two on in the ninth to end this epic, that Victorino's father headed for the clubhouse to tell him the sad news.

"I told my dad I'm going home for my grandma's funeral [in Hawaii]," Victorino said afterward, his eyes still red with grief. "I hope they can schedule it on an off-day, maybe. But right now, I want to be with this team, because that's my job, and it's important. I'm sure Charlie feels the same way. He wants to be there for his family. But he also wants to be there with this team."

However Charlie Manuel was feeling during Game 2, though, he left those feelings unspoken. He didn't address the media. He was unusually quiet all day in the dugout.

"At one point, around the fifth inning, I looked over and he was just pacing in the dugout," said Dobbs. "And I thought to myself, *I can't imagine what he's going through*. His mother just passed away. You've got 40,000 fans screaming their lungs out. And we're playing, at the time, the most important game of our season. And he's managing that game. I found myself trying to empathize, trying to put myself in his shoes. It had to be very difficult."

But the day kept reeling forward. And then there was Brad Lidge finishing off his 45th consecutive save, giving his team that 2–zilch lead, elevating the Phillies to a place where only three teams in LCS history have failed to reach the World Series—up 2–0 in a best-of-seven series. And fireworks popped overhead.

A dugout full of Phillies raced out of the dugout to celebrate. But for nearly a minute afterward, their manager didn't follow them.

Finally, Charlie Manuel hopped up those dugout steps and began shaking hands. Only when he was finished, when he had pumped every fist, did he turn and find Thompson there waiting for him. The hitting coach slipped his arm over his boss' shoulder. Then they headed for the clubhouse together.

"He's an incredible man," Thompson would say later, of his manager and friend. "It was just one of those moments where I was letting him know he'd made it through a tough day, but it's going to get better. It's rough right now. But it's going to get better."

In any other line of work when moments like this strike, you can stop the world, take a leave from your job, do what matters most for the family members around you. But not in this business. In this business, October stops for no one. Life goes on. Baseball goes on.

So Charlie Manuel would go on. He went on to the airplane to California. He went on to Game 3 and beyond. Some day, when the time was right and this series was over, he would make it back to Virginia and mourn the way he needed to mourn. But on this day, there was no time for that. He knew it, and his baseball team understood it.

"There's only so much sports can do to ease the pain," said Brett Myers. "But I hope we can help ease it—especially the guys in this club-house. We're all behind Charlie just as much as he's behind us. If he needs any of us for anything, we're there for him."

What he needed from Game 2—what they all needed—was the victory that propelled them closer to the sixth World Series appointment in franchise history. But this time, that victory was about more than just baseball.

They found themselves playing this game on a sparkling diamond inside a more meaningful circle. On this unforgettable day, the diamond that is baseball collided head on with the circle that is life.

NL Championship Series, Game 2,
October 10, 2008, at Philadelphia
Phillies 8, Dodgers 5

LA Dodgers	AB	R	H	RBI	BB	SO	LOB	AVG
Furcal, SS	5	1	1	0	0	2	0	.111
Martin, C	4	2	1	0	1	2	1	.286
Ramirez, M, LF	4	1	1	3	1	1	2	.375
Ethier, RF	4	1	1	0	1	2	1	.375
Loney, 1B	4	0	2	1	1	1	0	.429
Kemp, CF	3	0	0	0	2	2	4	.143
DeWitt, 2B	2	0	0	1	0	1	4	.000
McDonald, P	1	0	0	0	0	0	1	.000
a-Garciaparra, PH-3B	2	0	1	0	0	1	2	.500
Blake, 3B	3	0	1	0	1	0	3	.143
Kershaw, P	0	0	0	0	0	0	0	.000
Wade, P	0	0	0	0	0	0	0	.000
Billingsley, P	1	0	0	0	0	0	2	.000
Park, P	0	0	0	0	0	0	0	.000
Beimel, P	0	0	0	0	0	0	0	.000
Kent, 2B	3	0	0	0	0	0	1	.000
Totals	36	5	8	5	7	12	21	

Philadelphia	AB	R	H	RBI	BB	SO	LOB	AVG
Rollins, SS	5	1	1	0	0	4	4	.111
Victorino, CF	5	0	2	4	0	0	0	.222
Utley, 2B	1	0	0	0	4	0	0	.400
Howard, 1B	4	0	0	0	1	2	4	.000
Burrell, LF	4	0	1	0	0	3	4	.429
Bruntlett, LF	0	0	0	0	1	0	0	.000
Werth, RF	5	1	1	0	0	2	1	.125
Dobbs, 3B	3	2	2	0	1	1	0	.667
Romero, P	0	0	0	0	0	0	0	.000
Madson, P	0	0	0	0	0	0	0	.000
Lidge, P	0	0	0	0	0	0	0	.000
Ruiz, C	4	2	1	1	0	0	4	.429
Myers, P	3	2	3	3	0	0	0	1.000
Durbin, C, P	0	0	0	0	0	0	0	.000
Feliz, 3B	1	0	0	0	0	0	0	.000
Totals	35	8	11	8	7	12	17	

a-Singled for McDonald in the 7th.

BATTING
2B: Loney (1, Myers).
HR: Ramirez, M (1, 4th inning off Myers, 2 on, 2 out).
TB: Furcal; Martin; Ramirez, M 4; Ethier; Loney 3; Garciaparra; Blake.
RBI: DeWitt (2), Loney (1), Ramirez, M 3 (4).
2-out RBI: Loney; Ramirez, M 3.
Runners left in scoring position, 2 out: Billingsley; DeWitt 2; Blake; Garciaparra.
GIDP: Kent.
Team LOB: 11.

FIELDING
E: Kemp (1, fielding).

BATTING
2B: Ruiz (1, Billingsley), Werth (1, Billingsley).
3B: Victorino (1, Park).
TB: Rollins; Victorino 4; Burrell; Werth 2; Dobbs 2; Ruiz 2; Myers 3.
RBI: Ruiz (1), Myers 3 (3), Victorino 4 (4).
2-out RBI: Ruiz; Myers; Victorino 4.
Runners left in scoring position, 2 out: Howard; Burrell 3; Rollins.
Team LOB: 10.

FIELDING
E: Dobbs (1, fielding).
DP: (Rollins-Utley-Howard).

LA Dodgers	IP	H	R	ER	BB	SO	HR	ERA
Billingsley (L, 0-1)	2.1	8	8	7	3	5	0	27.00
Park	0.1	1	0	0	0	1	0	0.00
Beimel	0.0	0	0	0	2	0	0	0.00
McDonald	3.1	2	0	0	1	5	0	0.00
Kershaw	1.2	0	0	0	1	1	0	0.00
Wade	0.1	0	0	0	0	0	0	0.00

Philadelphia	IP	H	R	ER	BB	SO	HR	ERA
Myers (W, 1-0)	5.0	6	5	5	4	6	1	9.00
Durbin, C (H, 1)	1.0	1	0	0	0	0	0	0.00
Romero (H, 1)	0.2	0	0	0	1	1	0	0.00
Madson (H, 2)	1.1	1	0	0	0	2	0	0.00
Lidge (S, 2)	1.0	0	0	0	2	3	0	0.00

Beimel pitched to 2 batters in the 3rd.

WP: Myers; IBB: Dobbs (by Billingsley), Blake (by Myers); Pitches-strikes: Billingsley 59-36, Park 9-6, Beimel 12-4, McDonald 60-36, Kershaw 18-11, Wade 3-3, Myers 102-62, Durbin, C 10-6, Romero 13-8, Madson 14-11, Lidge 23-14; Groundouts-flyouts: Billingsley 1-1, Park 0-0, Beimel 0-0, McDonald 3-2, Kershaw 0-4, Wade 0-1, Myers 5-5, Durbin, C 0-3, Romero 1-0, Madson 1-1, Lidge 0-0; Batters faced: Billingsley 18, Park 2, Beimel 2, McDonald 13, Kershaw 6, Wade 1, Myers 26, Durbin, C 4, Romero 3, Madson 5, Lidge 5; Inherited runners-scored: Park 2-2, Beimel 1-0, McDonald 3-0, Wade 1-0, Romero 1-0. Umpires: HP: Jerry Meals. 1B: Mike Everitt. 2B: Ted Barrett. 3B: Mike Winters. LF: Gary Cederstrom. RF: Mike Reilly.

Weather: 74 degrees, sunny; Wind: 5 mph, Varies; T: 3:33; Att: 45,883.

Useless Information

- Welcome to an all–Brett Myers edition of Useless Info. Let's start here: His three RBIs in this game were two more than he drove in *all season*. That means—if we count only men who got at least 50 regular-season at-bats—he's just the second player ever to drive in more runs in the postseason than the entire regular season. The other, according to the Elias Sports Bureau: Blake Doyle, of the 1978 Yankees.

- Myers was the eighth pitcher in history to get three hits in a postseason game but only the third since 1924. The others: Dontrelle Willis in Game 4 of the 2003 NLDS and Orel Hershiser in Game 2 of the 1988 World Series.

- But here's a claim to fame nobody can match: Myers was the first player of all time to get three hits in a postseason game after batting under .100 during the regular season, according to Elias. He went 4-for-58 (.069) during the season.

- Since the DH era arrived in 1973, there have been only five other three-RBI games by pitchers in the postseason. The others: Tom Glavine in the 1996 NLCS, Mike Jackson in the 1995 NLDS, Steve Carlton in the 1978 NLCS, and Don Gullett twice—in both the 1975 and 1976 NLCS.

- Finally, there can't possibly have been any other player who ever saw 19 pitches in two at-bats in one postseason game (Game 2 of the NLDS), then swung at *every pitch thrown* the next game he played. But Brett Myers did it. I saw it with my own eyeballs.

Game 3: October 12, 2008

The Thrill of Victorino

LOS ANGELES—There are moments in the life of any good postseason series when everything changes.

And for a while there, Game 3 of the National League Championship Series felt like that moment. Specifically this:

A 94-mile-per-hour Hiroki Kuroda cannonball whizzing behind the noggin of Phillies center fielder Shane Victorino.

Before that pitch, in the third inning, this was just baseball. After that pitch, we didn't just have a series anymore. We had...*a series.*

A benches-emptying, fingers-wagging, neck-veins-bulging, coaches-jawing, Manny Manny-izing, crowd-shrieking, real-live, must-see-drama kind of series.

So this is from all of us must-see October drama fans to Hiroki Kuroda: Thanks for livening up the week.

When the day began, the Phillies were in total charge of this series, up two games to zip. Three hours—and one 7–2 Dodgers wipeout later—this was a whole different deal.

In the history of best-of-seven series, 35 teams have come back to win, down two games to one. But just one has roared back to win after tumbling into that 3–0 canyon. You can ask Joe Torre to tell you the story of that one sometime.

 But not on this night. On this night, we had more important matters to attend to. Like calling in some United Nations peace-keeping forces. Or Don King. Or both.

No haymakers ever did get thrown after Kuroda launched that fly-by in Victorino's airspace. But after Victorino then grounded out to first base and started yapping at Kuroda again, at least we got the thrill of having about 80 people in uniform charge onto the field for a lively conversation.

Manny Ramirez, in fact, proved to be a particularly engaging conversationalist. Heck, he was so engaging, it took a swarm of Dodgers to hold him in one place just so he could keep his gesticulations inside the 323 area code.

In the end, as violent sporting conflagrations go, it wasn't even up there with a good Kimbo Slice fiasco. But as Phillies reliever J.C. Romero so astutely assessed it, "It's part of the game. The ratings are up. Everybody is happy."

Well, not everybody. The Phillies weren't too happy to see their hard-earned LCS momentum disappear faster than you could say, "Biggest first inning in Dodgers postseason history" (i.e., five in the first off Jamie Moyer).

But the Dodgers appeared to brighten their mood considerably. After their pacifistic loss in Game 2, they were challenged by their manager to show more fight. So they made a statement in this game, in more ways than one.

"I think we needed this for ourselves, to go out and get some confidence that we're not going to be pushed around," said Dodgers catcher Russell Martin. "We're going to play the game the right way. Sometimes you've got to make a stand. And we got that done today."

But this was one stand they didn't just make on the old scoreboard.

From the second Brett Myers offered to trim Manny's dreadlocks with a straight-from-the-salon four-seam fastball in Game 2, it was only a matter of time before some sort of fun-filled imbroglio busted out in this series.

Dodgers players had been muttering about it for two days. One affectionately referred to Myers, between games, as a "wacko." And only a couple of hours before Game 3, right up there on the interview-room podium, Game 4 starter Derek Lowe suggested that it might be time to address this situation "Nuke LaLoosh style."

Well, no nukes ever did get dropped, but Kuroda clearly fired a warning shot over the brow of Victorino. And if this was a message, Victorino obviously got it.

He turned directly toward Kuroda and started pointing at his head, then his ribs, then his head again, as the largest crowd in Dodger Stadium history (56,800) began buzzing ecstatically. Afterward, however, Victorino had no interest in rehashing any of this. At one point, when a reporter pressed him on it one time too many, he retorted, "I'm done," and walked away.

But Martin, being the closest earwitness, reported, "He said, 'If you're going to hit me, hit me in the ribs. Don't hit me in the head.' But we weren't trying to hit anyone."

Whatever they *were* trying to do, though, give the Dodgers credit: They had their alibis down cold.

Kuroda spun out the old "It just slipped out of my hand" excuse. Manny could only guess that "Maybe the ball slipped." Matt Kemp at least did some minor creative editing, theorizing that "The ball just got away from him."

And if you believe any of that, we've got your own personal star on the Walk of Fame we'd like to sell you.

Jimmy Rollins strikes out in Game 3 of the National League Championship series against the Los Angeles Dodgers on October 12, 2008.

But after the Pitch, there was even better action to come. Victorino may have gotten his point across once, but he couldn't resist resuming the monologue after his inning-ending groundout, when Kuroda wandered within easy shouting distance.

Next thing they knew, everybody but Henry Winkler was charging toward the infield. And Manny turned on his heretofore-hidden Usain

Bolt jets, motored in from left field in record time, and got so overheated that he had to be restrained by Martin and coach Bob Schaefer before he…well, we're not sure what, exactly.

Asked if he was trying to get at anyone in particular, Ramirez reached into his Drew Rosenhaus quote book and answered, "Next."

Asked after that if he was yelling at anyone in particular, Manny stayed in rhythm and replied again, "Next."

If Martin knew the answer to those questions, he wasn't saying. But we have to say he displayed better gang-tackling form than the Oklahoma Sooners did this weekend. And he needed to, because Manny was showing off his full array of LaDanian Tomlinson escapability moves, as Martin hung on for dear life.

"He tried a spin move on me at one point," Martin reported. "Then I had ahold of his jersey a little bit…. He was definitely fired up. I don't know who he was trying to go after, but at least we kept him in the game."

Gee, we hate to break this to him, but Manny claimed later he actually *wanted* to be restrained.

"I don't want to fight nobody," Ramirez said. "I'm a lover, not a fighter."

He wasn't the only one making the highlight reels, however. Dodgers coach Larry Bowa, the former Phillie, and Phillies coach, Davey Lopes, the former Dodger, had quite the lovefest going themselves.

"Davey just said, 'You guys should have taken care of it [in Game 2],' and he's right," Bowa said. "He's 100 percent right…. He said, 'Let's play baseball.' And I said, 'Let's play baseball.' And that's right. I respect Davey. Davey was a great player."

"Nothing really happened," Lopes said. "Nobody got hurt. Nobody got thrown out. Somebody might have got their feelings hurt, but nothing really happened."

Ah, but that's where he's wrong. Something *definitely* happened on those exotic grass blades at Chavez Ravine during Game 3.

The Dodgers needed to win this game, for one thing. But that's not all they needed. They needed to show a little life, a little pulse, a little competitive fire. There were rumblings that after Game 2, they got an earful from both Joe Torre and their coaching staff. And not just about failing to retaliate for Brett Myers' little transgression, either. For going down so meekly after Ramirez had given them a second chance with a three-run homer.

Asked if the manager had suggested it was time to put up more of a fight, Martin diplomatically replied, "I don't know that he wanted us to show more fight. He keeps talking about playing the game right and being aggressive, and I think we did that tonight."

They mugged Moyer with a five-run first. They answered a Phillies run in the top of the second with a Rafael Furcal homer. They went first to third. They had just one 1-2-3 inning all night. They made big pitches and big plays any time the Phillies threatened. They finally looked again like that team that swept the Cubs—because they looked like a team, period.

"You have teammates," Torre said. "And you're there for your teammates. And you have to support them. And that's what I think a lot of this is all about."

So with Game 4 just around the bend the next day, at least they'd provided this series with a whole new dimension—intrigue.

The Wrestlemania portion of this series—that was over. But the riveting October drama had just begun. And that, come to think of it, was the whole idea.

NL Championship Series, Game 3,
October 12, 2008, at Los Angeles
Dodgers 7, Phillies 2

Philadelphia	AB	R	H	RBI	BB	SO	LOB	AVG
Rollins, SS	4	0	0	0	0	2	1	.077
Victorino, CF	4	0	0	0	0	0	1	.154
Utley, 2B	3	1	1	0	1	0	1	.375
Howard, 1B	4	1	2	0	0	0	0	.167
Burrell, LF	4	0	1	1	0	2	1	.364
Werth, RF	4	0	1	0	0	2	3	.167
Feliz, 3B	4	0	1	1	0	0	3	.143
Ruiz, C	2	0	0	0	0	1		.333
c-Dobbs, PH	1	0	0	0	0	0	2	.500
Durbin, C, P	0	0	0	0	0	0	0	.000
Romero, P	0	0	0	0	0	0	0	.000
Moyer, P	0	0	0	0	0	0	0	.000
Condrey, P	0	0	0	0	0	0	0	.000
a-Jenkins, PH	1	0	0	0	0	0	0	.000
Happ, P	0	0	0	0	0	0	0	.000
b-Taguchi, PH	1	0	0	0	0	0	0	.000
Eyre, P	0	0	0	0	0	0	0	.000
Coste, C	1	0	1	0	0	0	0	1.000
Totals	33	2	7	2	1	6	13	

a-Grounded out for Condrey in the 3rd. b-Grounded out for Happ in the 6th. c-Grounded out for Ruiz in the 7th.

BATTING
2B: Howard (1, Kuroda), Utley (1, Kuroda).
TB: Utley 2; Howard 3; Burrell; Werth; Feliz; Coste.
RBI: Feliz (1), Burrell (2).
2-out RBI: Feliz.
Runners left in scoring position, 2 out: Dobbs.
Team LOB: 5.

BASERUNNING
CS: Utley (1, 2nd base by Kuroda/Martin).

FIELDING
Outfield assists: Burrell (Martin at 3rd base).
DP: (Rollins-Utley-Howard).
Pickoffs: Happ (Kemp at 1st base).

LA Dodgers	AB	R	H	RBI	BB	SO	LOB	AVG
Furcal, SS	4	2	2	1	1	0	0	.231
Ethier, RF	5	1	1	0	0	1	1	.308
Ramirez, M, LF	2	2	1	1	2	0	0	.400
Martin, C	1	1	0	0	1	0	1	.250
Garciaparra, 1B	3	0	2	1	0	1	3	.600
a-Loney, PH-1B	1	0	0	0	0	1	1	.375
Blake, 3B	3	1	1	1	1	0	1	.200
Kemp, CF	4	0	2	0	0	2	5	.273
DeWitt, 2B	3	0	1	3	0	1	2	.125
Berroa, 2B	1	0	0	0	0	0	0	.000
Kuroda, P	3	0	0	0	0	1	3	.000
Wade, P	0	0	0	0	0	0	0	.000
b-Kent, PH	1	0	0	0	0	1	0	.000
Broxton, P	0	0	0	0	0	0	0	.000
Totals	31	7	10	7	5	8	17	

a-Struck out for Garciaparra in the 7th. b-Struck out for Wade in the 8th.

BATTING
3B: DeWitt (1, Moyer).
HR: Furcal (1, 2nd inning off Moyer, 0 on, 0 out).
TB: Furcal 5; Ethier; Ramirez, M; Garciaparra 2; Blake; Kemp 2; DeWitt 3.
RBI: Ramirez, M (5), Blake (1), DeWitt 3 (5), Furcal (1), Garciaparra (1).
2-out RBI: DeWitt 3; Garciaparra.
Runners left in scoring position, 2 out: Kuroda 2; Kemp.
GIDP: Martin.
Team LOB: 7.

BASERUNNING
SB: Martin (1, 2nd base off Durbin, C/Coste).
CS: Kemp (1, 2nd base by Happ/Ruiz).
PO: Kemp (1st base by Happ).

Philadelphia	IP	H	R	ER	BB	SO	HR	ERA
Moyer (L, 0-1)	1.1	6	6	6	0	2	1	40.50
Condrey	0.2	0	0	0	1	0	0	0.00
Happ	3.0	4	1	1	2	2	0	3.00
Eyre	1.0	0	0	0	0	0	0	0.00
Durbin, C	1.0	0	0	0	1	2	0	0.00
Romero	1.0	0	0	0	1	2	0	0.00

LA Dodgers	IP	H	R	ER	BB	SO	HR	ERA
Kuroda (W, 1-0)	6.0	5	2	2	1	3	0	3.00
Wade	2.0	1	0	0	0	2	0	0.00
Broxton	1.0	1	0	0	0	1	0	0.00

Kuroda pitched to 3 batters in the 7th.

HBP: Martin (by Moyer), Martin (by Durbin, C); Pitches-strikes: Moyer 32-22, Condrey 8-3, Happ 44-24, Eyre 9-7, Durbin, C 21-13, Romero 16-10, Kuroda 84-50, Wade 33-22, Broxton 14-10; Groundouts-flyouts: Moyer 1-1, Condrey 2-0, Happ 2-3, Eyre 2-1, Durbin, C 0-1, Romero 1-0, Kuroda 8-6, Wade 2-2, Broxton 1-1; Batters faced: Moyer 11, Condrey 2, Happ 13, Eyre 3, Durbin, C 5, Romero 4, Kuroda 23, Wade 7, Broxton 4; Inherited runners-scored: Wade 2-0; Umpires: HP: Mike Everitt. 1B: Ted Barrett. 2B: Mike Winters. 3B: Gary Cederstrom. LF: Mike Reilly. RF: Jerry Meals.

Weather: 70 degrees, clear; Wind: 9 mph, Out to CF; T: 2:57; Att: 56,800.

Useless
Information

- Before this game, the Phillies had played 63 postseason games in franchise history. The Dodgers had played 162. The Phillies had never allowed a five-run first inning. And the Dodgers had never scored five in the first. But all those streaks ended in the first inning of this game.

- This was the seventh postseason start of Jamie Moyer's career. He gave up only 10 earned runs in 33⅔ innings in the first six. He allowed five in just 1⅓ innings in this game.

- Moyer has been in the big leagues since 1986, but he did something in the first inning of this game he had done only one other time in all those years—he gave up a bases-loaded triple (to Blake DeWitt). The only other player to hit a three-run triple off Moyer in his career: Jose Offerman, on September 4, 2004.

- Moyer's four-out start was the third shortest postseason start in Phillies history. The only two that were shorter: Larry Christenson (⅓ IP) in Game 4 of the 1980 World Series and Bob Miller (also ⅓ IP) in Game 4 of the 1950 World Series.

- This was the 11th game played in 2008 between the Dodgers and Phillies. The home team won every one of those 11.

Game 4: October 13, 2005

Please Use
the Stairs

LOS ANGELES—The magic of October is that you can't script it, you can't predict it, you can't even explain it.

So who wrote this script? Who predicted this finish? Who can explain the unbelievable chain of events that would lead the Phillies to the brink of their first World Series journey in 15 years?

A game-winning pinch-hit home run by a 40-year-old guy who hadn't gotten a hit all month?

A game-losing, series-altering gopherball by a pitcher who hadn't served up a home run in his home ballpark in so long, the Dow had dropped about 5,000 points since then?

A game-tying homer by the biggest villain in town, a fellow who was about as popular in Los Angeles as gas prices?

A heart-pumping four-out save by a closer who hadn't gotten a four-out save since July 6, 2006?

And that, friends, is just the Cliffs Notes version of an October baseball game that will rattle around the memory banks for decades.

It was Game 4 of the National League Championship Series—a rampaging roller-coaster ride of a ballgame that spun your insides around for 3 hours, 44 spine-tingling minutes, until somehow, it wound up Phillies 7, Dodgers 5 on an unforgettable California evening.

So let's sum up quickly what this evening meant: It gave the Phillies the lead in the series, three games to one, with their best pitcher (Cole Hamels) lined up to pitch Game 5 and two games at home as their safety valve if they needed them.

In other words, this was a game that left them one win away from a shot at winning the second World Series in the 126 seasons in franchise history. But on a crazy night in Chavez Ravine, they were five outs away from a very different place.

They were five outs away from a crushing loss, a loss that would have evened this series at two wins apiece, a loss that would have brought all the tragic moments from their star-crossed history showering down on all their heads.

But this was a team that didn't think that way. This was a team that thought two-run eighth-inning deficits were just the perfect launching pad to kick off their latest miracle comeback.

"This team's amazing," said their closer, Brad Lidge, in a raucous October clubhouse. "I don't care if we're down by 10 runs. If there's two innings left, we just believe that somehow, some way, we're going to catch up. No matter how many runs we're down by, I'm still thinking I'm going to come into the game."

This was their sixth win of the year in a game they trailed by two runs or more in the eighth inning or later. But nobody could top this comeback on their all-time degree-of-difficulty list.

By the time L.A's least favorite Phillie, Shane Victorino, headed for home plate in the eighth, his team had already blitzed through the heart of its bullpen, blown out most of its bench, coughed up an early two-run lead, and dug a two-run sixth-inning hole on a gruesome Ryan Howard error. Little did the Dodgers know this team had them right where it wanted them, right?

"That's what it's about," Victorino would say later, that heart still thumping with excitement. "It's about 25 guys going out there and never giving up. I mean, look at tonight. I can't even say who was left on the bench. I think [Chris Coste] was our only guy. And who was left in the bullpen—was it just [Clay] Condrey and [J.A.] Happ? But that's the kind of game it was. It was worrying about what was going on at the moment."

And what was going on at the moment Victorino dug in against reliever Cory Wade was exactly what was going on for two crazy days in L.A.: *Booooooooooooooooooooooooo.*

The man who took on Hiroki Kuroda—and, by extension, the entire population of the Los Angeles metropolitan area, right down to Barbra Streisand—during Game 3 wasn't a good candidate to run for mayor of L.A. at that point. And his Flyin' Hawaiian bobble figurine didn't figure to be a real hot item, either, come to think of it.

"Yeah it would," said Victorino's buddy, Jimmy Rollins. "So they could throw it off the top of the ravine."

But if Victorino was that beloved before that at-bat, he elevated himself to the Villain of the Century one pitch later.

Wade—a fellow who hadn't given up a home run to any of the previous 84 hitters he'd faced, dating all the way back to August 28—hung a breaking ball. And Victorino sliced it through the California night, toward deep right field. Was it going to drop? Was it going to carry to the track? Was it going to clank off the fence? Was it—huh?—somehow flying right over the bullpen gate and tying this game? Yep. Sure was.

"It's funny," said Lidge, one of the few remaining occupants of the Phillies' bullpen, of the moment he saw that baseball heading his way. "I'd actually just told J.A. Happ that Shane was about to hit a double down the line. And Happ about freaked out when that ball was halfway

Geoff Jenkins, left, and Pat Burrell congratulate Matt Stairs after Stairs hit a two-run home run in the eighth inning of Game 4 of the National League Championship Series on October 13, 2008.

out there. Then it cleared the fence, and we both freaked out. It only missed [catcher] Lou Marson's head by about six inches."

Victorino pumped his fist emotionally on a frantic, pulse-racing trip around the bases. The Phillies' bench looked like Mardi Gras had just busted out. And every decibel of noise seemed to be vacuumed out of shell-shocked Dodger Stadium.

Even up in the clubhouse, where a group of already-used Phillies pitchers were watching on TV, *shock* was the operative word.

"The crazy thing is," said left-hander Scott Eyre, "is that, honestly, we talked about it in the bullpen. Chad Durbin said, 'Wouldn't it be unbelievable if Shane hit one into the bullpen after what happened the last couple of days?' And wouldn't you know, he did?"

As Victorino sprinted around the bases, Rollins said the only thing he could think of was a story Willie Mays told when they were both guests on a *Costas Now* HBO show this summer. He couldn't remember every detail—just the part about how the fans kept booing Mays and Mays kept driving in runs until "the announcer came over the loudspeaker and said, 'Please stop booing, 'cause he's killing us.'"

But in reality, it wasn't Shane Victorino's homer that was the killer. All his home run did was downgrade the Dodgers to guarded, but stable condition, because even after it landed, this game was only tied. It would actually be the next home run that kicked the Dodgers over the cliff.

And the next home run came three hitters later, in an even less likely scenario. With two outs and Carlos Ruiz on first, veteran let-it-fly pinch-hitter Matt Stairs popped out into the on-deck circle. So even though it was only the eighth inning, Joe Torre waved for his closer, the almost-unhittable Jonathan Broxton.

And why wouldn't he? Broxton had faced 16 hitters this October—and given up a hit to precisely one of them. So while this wasn't quite the same thing as Torre waving for the Great Mariano, it was as close as he could get in the Pacific Time Zone.

Stairs, meanwhile, wasn't quite Kirk Gibson, staggering toward home plate. But he hadn't exactly been doing much of a Reggie Jackson impression this October, either.

He'd batted precisely two times in this postseason—the last time eight days earlier. He had zero hits. And, thanks to a double-play ball, he'd produced more outs (three) than plate appearances (two).

This wasn't his first October rodeo. But in his three career trips to the postseason—with the '95 Red Sox, the 2000 A's, and this year's Phillies—he was only 1-for-12. His last hit was a double off Orlando (El Duque) Hernandez—eight years ago.

But this, said Rollins, "is why we brought him here."

Yep. He was in this time and place because the Phillies claimed him on waivers from the Blue Jays and were able to work out a trade on August 30, barely before the postseason-eligibility deadline. So here he was, a man who hadn't played a single game for this team before September 1, about to rewrite Phillies history.

He worked the count to 3-and-1. So Broxton reached back and did what he had to do: Fired his best 95-mph inferno right down the middle and dared Matt Stairs to hit it.

At his best, Broxton can be so untouchable that "you can get a ball like that a thousand times—and *hit* a ball like that maybe like 10 times," Rollins said. "But tonight was that night. He hit it."

Yeah, Matt Stairs hit it, all right. He hit it so high and so far to deep right field that at first, said Howard, "I thought it was going to leave the park and hit the roof." Instead, it "only" came down two-thirds of the way up the right-field pavilion—a mammoth blast in this park. And as that baseball finally settled to earth, folks from Chavez Ravine to

Cheltenham needed a moment—or maybe an eternity—to make sense of what they'd all just witnessed.

You have to go all the way back to Tito Landrum, of the 1983 Orioles, to find a player who hit a game-winning October home run this late in a game after not playing a single game for his team before August 31.

And you won't find anybody—anybody *ever*—who hit a postseason home run of this magnitude after playing as few regular-season games for their team as Stairs did for this team (16).

Meanwhile, Broxton hadn't given up a home run—to anybody, any-where—since May 31. That was 217 hitters ago. And he hadn't served up a home run in this park—his park—since July 24, 2006.

So how did this happen, exactly? How was this possible—this epic homer by a 40-year-old man who'd been sitting around watching for three hours?

"Hey, have you followed Matt Stairs' career?" laughed reliever J.C. Romero. "Everyone knows what he's capable of doing—at 20, at 30, at 40. If you throw him a fastball, he can make you look real bad."

And he can do that because he has just one mission in life every time he heads for home plate: "I'm not going to lie," said Matt Stairs. "I try to hit home runs. And that's it."

But of all those home runs he's hit—all 254 of them—there has never been one like this one. An October game-winner off one of the best closers in America? At 40 years old? This one, Stairs said, "is definitely the top pinch-hit home run of my career."

Just don't call it a dream come true. Asked if he'd ever dreamed of hitting *this* home run, Stairs thought he'd better remind the world of something important: He's a Canadian.

"Welllllll," he chuckled, "I've probably been dreaming of scoring on a breakaway. In case you didn't know, I'm kind of a big hockey fan."

Okay, sorry. This was no frigging Stanley Cup. But it was a stunning October moment, a fittingly Hollywood shocker to decide a remarkable October baseball game.

But even the best scriptwriters in town couldn't have dreamed this one up. Shane Victorino and Matt Stairs hitting the home runs that shook the world?

"Hey, the postseason makes heroes, man," said Scott Eyre. "When you do it in the postseason, everyone knows who you are."

NL Championship Series, Game 4, October 13, 2008, at Los Angeles
Phillies 7, Dodgers 5

Philadelphia	AB	R	H	RBI	BB	SO	LOB	AVG
Rollins, SS	4	1	1	0	1	1	1	.118
Werth, RF	5	1	1	0	0	2	1	.176
Utley, 2B	5	0	3	1	0	2	0	.462
Howard, 1B	4	2	1	1	1	0	3	.188
Burrell, LF	3	0	1	0	1	0	2	.357
Bruntlett, LF	1	0	0	0	0	0	1	.000
Victorino, CF	3	1	1	2	0	0	2	.188
Dobbs, 3B	2	0	1	0	0	0	0	.500
a-Feliz, PH-3B	2	0	0	0	0	0	2	.111
Ruiz, C	3	1	2	0	1	0	1	.417
Blanton, P	2	0	0	0	0	2	2	.000
b-Jenkins, PH	0	0	0	0	0	0	0	.000
c-Taguchi, PH	1	0	0	0	0	0	2	.000
Durbin, C, P	0	0	0	0	0	0	0	.000
Eyre, P	0	0	0	0	0	0	0	.000
Madson, P	0	0	0	0	0	0	0	.000
d-Stairs, PH	1	1	1	2	0	0	0	1.000
Romero, P	0	0	0	0	0	0	0	.000
Lidge, P	0	0	0	0	0	0	0	.000
Totals	36	7	12	6	4	7	17	

LA Dodgers	AB	R	H	RBI	BB	SO	LOB	AVG
Furcal, SS	2	2	1	0	2	0	1	.267
Ethier, RF	5	1	1	0	0	0	4	.278
Ramirez, M, LF	2	0	2	1	3	0	0	.500
Martin, C	5	0	0	1	0	2	7	.154
Loney, 1B	4	0	2	1	1	1	2	.417
DeWitt, 2B	3	0	0	0	1	0	6	.091
Berroa, 2B	0	0	0	0	0	0	0	.000
b-Garciaparra, PH	1	0	0	0	0	0	0	.500
Blake, 3B	5	1	2	1	0	3	0	.267
Pierre, CF	3	1	2	0	0	0	0	.667
Kuo, P	0	0	0	0	0	0	0	.000
Wade, P	0	0	0	0	0	0	0	.000
Broxton, P	0	0	0	0	0	0	0	.000
c-Kent, PH	1	0	0	0	0	0	0	.000
Lowe, P	2	0	1	0	0	1	0	.250
Kershaw, P	0	0	0	0	0	0	0	.000
Park, P	0	0	0	0	0	0	0	.000
Beimel, P	0	0	0	0	0	0	0	.000
a-Kemp, PH-CF	1	0	0	0	1	0	2	.250
Totals	34	5	11	4	8	7	22	

a-Flied out for Dobbs in the 6th. b-Batted for Blanton in the 6th. c-Flied out for Jenkins in the 6th. d-Homered for Madson in the 8th.

a-Walked for Beimel in the 6th. b-Flied out for Berroa in the 9th. c-Lined out for Broxton in the 9th.

BATTING
2B: Utley (2, Lowe), Dobbs (1, Lowe).
HR: Victorino (1, 8th inning off Wade, 1 on, 1 out), Stairs (1, 8th inning off Broxton, 1 on, 2 out).
TB: Rollins; Werth; Utley 4; Howard; Burrell; Victorino 4; Dobbs 2; Ruiz 2; Stairs 4.
RBI: Utley (3), Howard (1), Victorino 2 (6), Stairs 2 (2).
2-out RBI: Stairs 2.
Runners left in scoring position, 2 out: Rollins; Taguchi; Werth.
S: Victorino.
GIDP: Victorino.
Team LOB: 7.

BATTING
2B: Loney (2, Blanton), Pierre (1, Durbin, C), Ramirez, M (2, Lidge).
HR: Blake (1, 6th inning off Durbin, C, 0 on, 0 out).
TB: Furcal; Ethier; Ramirez, M 3; Loney 3; Blake 5; Pierre 3; Lowe.
RBI: Loney (2), Ramirez, M (6), Martin (1), Blake (2).
2-out RBI: Loney.
Runners left in scoring position, 2 out: DeWitt 3; Kemp 2; Loney.
S: Furcal; Kuo.
GIDP: DeWitt; Ethier.
Team LOB: 12.

BASERUNNING
SB: Rollins (1, 2nd base off Broxton/Martin).
CS: Bruntlett (1, 2nd base by Broxton/Martin).

BASERUNNING
CS: Pierre (1, 2nd base by Blanton/Ruiz).

FIELDING
E: Howard (1, throw).
DP: 3 (Utley-Rollins-Howard, Utley, Rollins-Howard).

FIELDING
DP: (DeWitt-Furcal-Loney).

Philadelphia	IP	H	R	ER	BB	SO	HR	ERA
Blanton	5.0	7	3	3	4	4	0	5.40
Durbin, C	0.0	2	2	1	1	0	1	4.50
Eyre	0.1	0	0	0	1	0	0	0.00
Madson (W, 1-0)	1.2	1	0	0	1	1	0	0.00
Romero (H, 2)	0.2	0	0	0	1	0	0	0.00
Lidge (S, 3)	1.1	1	0	0	0	2	0	0.00

LA Dodgers	IP	H	R	ER	BB	SO	HR	ERA
Lowe	5.0	6	2	2	1	4	0	3.48
Kershaw (H, 1)	0.1	1	1	1	1	0	0	4.50
Park (BS, 1)	0.1	0	0	0	1	0	0	0.00
Beimel	0.1	0	0	0	0	0	0	0.00
Kuo (H, 1)	1.0	1	1	1	0	2	0	4.50
Wade (BS, 1) (L, 0-1)	0.2	2	2	2	0	0	1	6.00
Broxton	1.1	2	1	1	1	1	1	3.86

Durbin, C pitched to 3 batters in the 6th; Kuo pitched to 1 batter in the 8th; WP: Lidge, Park; IBB: Ramirez, M (by Blanton), Loney (by Blanton), Ramirez, M (by Eyre); Pitches-strikes: Blanton 91-53, Durbin, C 14-6, Eyre 14-7, Madson 20-14, Romero 6-2, Lidge 24-18, Lowe 74-51, Kershaw 14-7, Park 7-3, Beimel 1-1, Kuo 14-11, Wade 6-6, Broxton 30-17; Groundouts-flyouts: Blanton 6-4, Durbin, C 0-0, Eyre 0-1, Madson 1-2, Romero 2-0, Lidge 0-3, Lowe 8-3, Kershaw 1-0, Park 0-1, Beimel 0-1, Kuo 1-0, Wade 0-2, Broxton 2-0; Batters faced: Blanton 24, Durbin, C 3, Eyre 3, Madson 6, Romero 2, Lidge 6, Lowe 21, Kershaw 3, Park 2, Beimel 1, Kuo 4, Wade 4, Broxton 6; Inherited runners-scored: Eyre 2-1, Madson 3-0, Park 2-1, Beimel 2-0, Wade 1-1, Broxton 1-1 Umpires: HP: Ted Barrett. 1B: Mike Winters. 2B: Gary Cederstrom. 3B: Mike Reilly. LF: Jerry Meals. RF: Mike Everitt.

Weather: 74 degrees, clear; Wind: 8 mph, Varies; T: 3:44; Att: 56,800.

Useless
Information

- Shane Victorino's game-tying home run gave him 11 RBIs just in the first two rounds of this postseason. That's more postseason RBIs than Alex Rodriguez has had in 94 at-bats and 110 plate appearances in his five years with the Yankees.

- When Matt Stairs says he has never hit a home run quite like this one, he's not kidding. He's barely even come close. In the nine regular seasons from 2000–2008, Stairs hit just one other pinch homer in the eighth inning or later to give his team a lead—off the Reds' Todd Coffey on June 27, 2006.

- At age 40, Stairs was the oldest player in history to hit a pinch-hit postseason homer, according to the Elias Sports Bureau. The former record-holder? Johnny Mize, at age 39, in the 1952 World Series.

- Stairs' rocket was also the first go-ahead postseason home run hit by any player against the Dodgers in the eighth inning or later since Jack Clark's unforgettable series-ender off Tom Niedenfuer in the 1985 NLCS.

- The Dodgers lost just two games all year (68–2) when they led by two runs or more in the eighth inning or later. The Phillies won only five games all year (5–54) when they trailed by at least two runs in the eighth or later. But those trends sure didn't mean a whole lot in this game.

Game 5: October 15, 2008

Now It's
Their Turn

LOS ANGELES—They've spent their whole careers hearing about the Phillies of Carlton and Schmidt, the Phillies of Kruk and Dykstra, even the Phillies of Ashburn and Roberts. But now it's their turn.

Now it's Jimmy Rollins' Phillies. And Chase Utley's Phillies. And Cole Hamels' Phillies. Now it's Ryan Howard's Phillies. And Shane Victorino's Phillies. And even Matt Stairs' Phillies.

They play for a franchise that has witnessed more heartbreak than glory years. But now they've written their own story—a story they were determined to write, a story that finally led them to a World Series all their own.

"Now," said Rollins, on one of the most fulfilling nights of his baseball life, "we've finally got a chance to make our own mark."

They sent Manny Ramirez and that team from L.A. home on this night, finishing off a five-game NLCS blitzkrieg with a 5–1 win they led for all but seven pitches.

Fittingly, it was Rollins who started it, waving that magic, start-me-up wand of his with a stunning leadoff homer—the second time he'd kicked off a series-clinching win with a home-run trot just in this postseason.

And fittingly, it was the Phillies' impeccable closer, Brad Lidge, who finished it, snapping off one last bat-chomping slider that Nomar Garciaparra lofted into the California night.

And as that baseball floated through the sky, a soft-spoken catcher from Panama settled under it, asking himself for what seemed like an hour, *Is this thing ever going to come down?*

"I know that ball was not a tough play, but it took a long time," said Carlos Ruiz, after history had finally settled in his glove. "I was saying, 'Come on, baby. Let's go. Come down already.'"

But fortunately for him and that team he plays for, gravity was on all their sides. Eventually, that baseball returned to earth. And the Phillies were headed for a place they'd spent most of their lives watching everybody else go but them.

"I don't know if I understand what's really taken place here," said Jamie Moyer, the only member of this team who actually attended the parade of the only World Series champions in Phillies history. "I don't know if it's really sunk in. I know we're going to the World Series, but it hasn't sunk in."

With eyes watering, Moyer began to tell the story of what it was like to be a kid in high school in October 1980, skipping school to watch the champs parade down Broad Street.

"I remember people hanging from the streetlights and the trees, and toilet paper all over," Moyer said. "And everybody was your friend. A half a million people were all friends."

And then somehow, in 2006, the world spun and brought him back to his hometown, to a team that was still trying to figure out how to win these kinds of games. And a couple of weeks later, he found himself in the middle of a team meeting, telling his new friends about that parade—and laying out a dream for all of them, to reach a parade of their own someday.

"And now we're one series away from being on the floats in that parade," said Jamie Moyer. "It's amazing."

But for most of these men, nights like this had always been for all those other teams. For most of their careers, all they heard about themselves was that they couldn't win, wouldn't win, didn't know how to win.

They were the team that always chased somebody—the Braves, the Astros, the Mets, the Marlins—to the finish line but never broke that tape. Somebody else always did the celebrating. They were the ones trying to explain what happened.

"We always had good players, but we just couldn't seem to put it together," said Rollins. "There was always a piece missing."

But as the pieces began to fit together in the winter of 2006–07, it was Jimmy Rollins who stepped forward to change everything. He did it with one little quotation: "We *are* the team to beat."

The reverberations that erupted that day are still rumbling all these months later. And as the Moët & Chandon dripped down his face on this night, Jimmy Rollins thought back to the moment those prophetic words flowed out of his vocal cords. If he hadn't, he honestly believes this World Series journey might never have arrived.

"People thought I was crazy. Put it that way," Rollins said. "Even some of my teammates. That's the way it always is. People believe, but no one ever wants to say it. No one ever wants to make a statement and put himself out there. So I knew, when I answered the question, it was going to resonate in this clubhouse. And that's what I wanted. I really wanted to catch these guys' attention.

"This was an organization that wasn't used to winning. So saying things like that was definitely out of the ordinary.... But no one ever really said anything to catch guys' attention. And I thought, *Maybe we need to change that a little bit.*"

Chase Utley slides home safely as catcher Russell Martin can't make the catch on a wild throw from shortstop Rafael Furcal in Game 5 of the National League Championship Series on October 15, 2008.

People thought at the time that he uttered those words to throw a lightning bolt at the Mets. But what he really intended was to throw a jolt into another clubhouse—his own. To raise the bar. To change the mind-set. To transform the brainwaves when it came time to play the Big Games.

"That's what we had to do—change the way we approached the game, change the way we thought about it," Rollins said. "We were always a team with talent. We were always a team of underdogs. We were always a team that ran the bases well. But I wanted to be known as a team that *wins* well."

We know now how 2007 turned out for the Team to Beat. We know about the miracle finish to catch the Mets. We know about the painful first-round sweep by the Rockies. But what we couldn't know then was how that sweep led them to this place. How it gave them a different sense of purpose than any Phillies team in many, many years.

It was a sense of purpose that reminded reliever Chad Durbin of the 2006 Tigers World Series team he played for—except here, he said, "There's even more purpose. In Detroit, those guys were only together a little while. Here, the core of this team has been together for a lot of years."

Rollins and Pat Burrell arrived in 2000. Brett Myers checked in in 2002. Utley showed up in 2003. Howard and Victorino joined the mix in 2005, followed by ace of the future Cole Hamels in 2006.

Every year, they seemed to add another piece, get just a little closer. And that brought them to this year. To a year in which they roared out of the gates, took a seven-and-a-half-game lead over the Mets in mid-June, kicked away all seven and a half games of that lead in not much more than a month, and then, just when everyone else had kissed their chances good-bye, fired up their September magic carpet for the second straight year.

They went 13–3 down the stretch, blew by the Mets, wiped out the Brewers in the NLDS, and kept on charging—until they were one win from the World Series on a gorgeous October evening in Chavez Ravine.

And that was when the shortstop stalked up to home plate in the first inning and did exactly what he'd done a week and a half earlier in Milwaukee. He'd been thinking about this at-bat for a while, he said, thinking about how he could get this party started.

"I always do," Rollins said. "The night before, I always sit in bed and think. I stand in front of the mirror and practice my swing. A lot of things go through your mind. You know what people are going to throw. You know the way they pitch you. And you try to figure out a way to get it started."

As he worked the count to 2-and-2 off Dodgers starter Chad Billingsley, Rollins stepped out of the box and let his mind race some more. If he could just get that count to 3-and-2, he thought, *I know he'll have to throw me a fastball.*

He "thought about what happened in Milwaukee" and backed off the plate an inch or two. Sure enough, Billingsley launched that full-count fastball. As it began to tail over the middle of the plate, Rollins' eyes popped, his bat flashed, and the baseball disappeared over the right-field fence. It was 1–0 eight pitches into the game, and the World Series Express was rolling.

Soon that lead grew to 2–0. And 3–0. And then there was Dodgers shortstop Rafael Furcal conjuring up his inner Enzo Hernandez and becoming only the second player in postseason history to commit three errors in one inning. (Another Dodger, Willie Davis, was the other, back in 1966.)

Suddenly, it was Phillies 5, Dodgers 0, in the fifth. And with Hamels on the mound, spinning off zeroes, these men knew what that meant. They were about to win the biggest baseball game of their lives.

Ryan Madson—the set-up man who had given up exactly two earned runs in his last 21 trips to the mound—arrived to pitch the eighth. And the men in the dugout began counting down the outs.

"We had six outs to go, and I had the utmost confidence in our bullpen," said Moyer. "But those were six big outs, the six biggest outs of our season."

Turned out, however, that they were no problem. Madson blitzed through the eighth. Then Lidge burst out of the bullpen gates in the bottom of the ninth.

James Loney blooped a leadoff single. But down went Casey Blake for one out. Down went Matt Kemp for two outs. And then there was Garciaparra, flailing at one last slider. And there was that final pop-up hanging in the ozone, as one very nervous catcher waited for it to return to planet earth.

As a boy in Panama, Carlos Ruiz once watched these scenes on his television. Watched other catchers gather up these final outs in the defining games of their lives. Watched those other catchers land in frozen October moments, preserved through the magic of digital photography.

And then, he said, finding this hard to believe, "it happened to me."

He stuffed that baseball into his back pocket, ran right at Lidge, and leaped into his arms. Then he dissolved into a sea of grown men hugging each other for what seemed like a week.

These men play baseball in a town where, for 25 excruciating years, the only excuse to hold a parade had involved a bunch of banjo-strumming folks in feathers celebrating the new year (possibly because it had to beat the heck out of the old year where, once again, not one stinking team had won anything).

And so, as the drought dragged ever onward, the images of the Phillies teams that *had* won something, or at least came close, grew bigger, grew brighter, grew larger in the rearview mirror than they'd even seemed at the time.

"We've been hearing about that 1993 team and that 1980 team over and over again," said Rollins.

"Every time we get in a rain delay," Durbin laughed, "it's on six channels."

But now, everything's different. Now *they're* one of those teams. Now they're the team bound for a Rain Delay Theater highlight-film presentation on some rainy Thursday evening in 2016. And as the champagne flowed and the smiles glittered in the L.A. night, there was nothing harder for these men to comprehend than that.

"You know what? It hasn't hit me yet," Rollins said. "We still have a lot of work to do. We've got to find a way to win four more games. That's our goal. Our goal is to win the World Series. The goal was not just to win the National League. The goal was not just to get to the World Series. We qualified. That's all we did. So we've still got work to do.

"But when it's all said and done, and my career's over, and hopefully we win the World Series, then that legend of the Phillies in 2008 will be a great story. But until then, we've still got four games to win."

They felt like the hardest four games they'd ever tried to win. But even as they celebrated in the middle of a ball field 3,000 miles from home, the 2008 Phillies were still clinging as hard as ever to the sense of purpose that has made them what they are.

"We've gone this far," said Jamie Moyer. So why stop here?"

NL Championship Series, Game 5, October 15, 2008, at Los Angeles
Phillies 5, Dodgers 1

Philadelphia	AB	R	H	RBI	BB	SO	LOB	AVG
Rollins, SS	4	2	1	1	1	1	0	.143
Werth, RF	4	0	1	0	1	1	1	.190
Utley, 2B	4	2	0	0	1	2	2	.353
Howard, 1B	4	1	3	1	1	0	0	.300
Burrell, LF	4	0	1	1	0	1	1	.333
Bruntlett, LF	1	0	0	0	0	0	1	.000
Victorino, CF	2	0	1	0	2	1	0	.222
Feliz, 3B	4	0	1	0	0	2	8	.154
Ruiz, C	4	0	0	0	0	0	3	.313
Hamels, P	3	0	0	0	0	2	3	.200
a-Taguchi, PH	1	0	0	0	0	0	0	.000
Madson, P	0	0	0	0	0	0	0	.000
Lidge, P	0	0	0	0	0	0	0	.000
Totals	35	5	8	3	6	10	19	

LA Dodgers	AB	R	H	RBI	BB	SO	LOB	AVG
Furcal, SS	4	0	0	0	0	0	0	.211
Ethier, RF	4	0	0	0	0	1	0	.227
Ramirez, M, LF	3	1	2	1	1	0	0	.533
Martin, C	4	0	0	0	0	1	2	.118
Loney, 1B	4	0	2	0	0	1	0	.438
Blake, 3B-2B	4	0	1	0	0	0	2	.263
Kemp, CF	3	0	2	0	1	0	1	.333
DeWitt, 2B	2	0	0	0	0	0	4	.077
McDonald, P	0	0	0	0	0	0	0	.000
c-Garciaparra,								
PH-3B	1	0	0	0	1	0	1	.429
Billingsley, P	0	0	0	0	0	0	0	.000
Park, P	1	0	0	0	0	0	0	.000
a-Ozuna, PH	1	0	0	0	0	0	0	.000
Maddux, P	0	0	0	0	0	0	0	.000
b-Kent, PH-2B	2	0	0	0	0	2	3	.000
Beimel, P	0	0	0	0	0	0	0	.000
Wade, P	0	0	0	0	0	0	0	.000
Kuo, P	0	0	0	0	0	0	0	.000
Totals	32	1	7	1	3	5	13	

a-Grounded out for Hamels in the 8th.

BATTING
HR: Rollins (1, 1st inning off Billingsley, 0 on, 0 out).
TB: Rollins 4; Werth; Howard 3; Burrell; Victorino; Feliz.
RBI: Rollins (1), Howard (2), Burrell (3).
2-out RBI: Howard; Burrell.
Runners left in scoring position, 2 out: Feliz 2; Hamels 2; Ruiz.
GIDP: Utley; Bruntlett.
Team LOB: 9.

BASERUNNING
SB: Rollins (2, 2nd base off Billingsley/Martin).

FIELDING
DP: 2 (Utley-Rollins-Howard 2).

a-Bunted out for Park in the 3rd. b-Struck out for Maddux in the 5th. c-Walked for McDonald in the 7th.

BATTING
HR: Ramirez, M (2, 6th inning off Hamels, 0 on, 2 out).
TB: Ramirez, M 5; Loney 2; Blake; Kemp 2.
RBI: Ramirez, M (7).
2-out RBI: Ramirez, M.
Runners left in scoring position, 2 out: Kent 2; Martin; Garciaparra.
GIDP: DeWitt 2.
Team LOB: 7.

FIELDING
E: Furcal 3 (4, fielding, throw, throw).
DP: 2 (Loney-Furcal, Blake-Furcal-Loney).

Philadelphia	IP	H	R	ER	BB	SO	HR	ERA
Hamels (W, 2-0)	7.0	5	1	1	3	5	1	1.93
Madson	1.0	1	0	0	0	0	0	0.00
Lidge	1.0	1	0	0	0	0	0	0.00

Tampa Bay	IP	H	R	ER	BB	SO	HR	ERA
Billingsley (L, 0-2)	2.2	4	3	3	4	4	1	18.00
Park	0.1	0	0	0	0	0	0	0.00
Maddux	2.0	2	2	0	1	3	0	0.00
McDonald	2.0	1	0	0	1	2	0	0.00
Beimel	0.1	0	0	0	0	0	0	0.00
Wade	0.2	0	0	0	0	0	0	4.91
Kuo	1.0	1	0	0	0	1	0	3.00

WP: Billingsley; IBB: Victorino (by Billingsley), Victorino (by Maddux); Pitches-strikes: Hamels 104-68, Madson 15-12, Lidge 19-10, Billingsley 66-36, Park 2-2, Maddux 38-24, McDonald 29-18, Beimel 3-2, Wade 8-6, Kuo 13-8; Groundouts-flyouts: Hamels 10-6, Madson 1-2, Lidge 0-3, Billingsley 3-1, Park 1-0, Maddux 2-1, McDonald 3-1, Beimel 1-0, Wade 2-0, Kuo 2-0. Batters faced: Hamels 27, Madson 4, Lidge 4, Billingsley 15, Park 1, Maddux 11, McDonald 8, Beimel 1, Wade 2, Kuo 3. Inherited runners-scored: Park 3-0; Umpires: HP: Mike Winters. 1B: Gary Cederstrom. 2B: Mike Reilly. 3B: Jerry Meals. LF: Mike Everitt. RF: Ted Barrett.

Weather: 89 degrees, partly cloudy; Wind: 6 mph, Out to RF; T: 3:14; Att: 56,800.

Useless
Information

- Another clincher, another leadoff homer by Jimmy Rollins. He's the first player in history with two leadoff home runs in the same postseason—let alone two in two series-clinching games in the same postseason.

- Amazingly, Rollins hit as many leadoff homers in this postseason as he hit during the regular season (two). They gave him 34 leadoff bombs altogether in his career. He'd hit *nine* the year before, plus one in the 2007 postseason.

- Cole Hamels (24 years, 10 months old) was the second-youngest starting pitcher ever to win a series-clinching game against the Dodgers. The youngest: Dave McNally of the Orioles (at 23 years, 11 months) in the 1966 World Series.

- Before he ever even qualified for arbitration (or was finished pitching in this postseason), Hamels had already won more postseason games (three) than any pitcher in Phillies history who wasn't named Steve Carlton. (Carlton won six.) In fact, the only other Phillies with two postseason wins who weren't members of this team were both relievers—Mitch Williams and Tug McGraw.

- Half the teams in baseball—15 of 30—made it to the World Series in the 15 years between Phillies visits to the World Series.

Part 5
The World Series

A week off in October is a great thing for you or me. For us, a week off in October means sneaking off for a golf trip, or a peaceful week on the beach, or a jaunt through the wonders of some new European destination. But a week off in October for a baseball team? Not such a great thing. Not usually. Ask the 2007 Rockies. Ask the 2006 Tigers. One minute they were riding a miraculous October wave. The next, they'd forgotten how to hit, forgotten how to win, even forgotten how to throw a baseball to first base.

So a week between October baseball games could have been the twist of fate that did in the 2008 Phillies. But it wasn't. Or the wrath of the weather gods could have been the death knell of the 2008 Phillies. Who among us doubts it would have been in any other October? But not in this October.

CC Sabathia couldn't squash this team. Manny Ramirez couldn't squish this team. A week in Philadelphia weather hell nearly drowned this team, but it couldn't stop this group from fulfilling a mission that seemed to drive them all from Day One of spring training.

So in the end, even the weather turned into their friend. Yeah, it didn't seem like it at the time. But as Game 5, Part 2 of this World Series was about to resume, something happened that nobody seemed to notice—or at least something that nobody else seemed to make a big deal of: The Phillies headed out for batting practice—before the sixth inning—dressed like a team getting ready to play baseball. The Rays, on the other hand, came out bundled up like a team getting ready to watch the Olympic bobsled trials. In other words, one team was ready to play; the other was just trying to survive.

And that, in a way, was the story of the 2008 postseason. The team with the greater sense of purpose won the World Series. But of course, as we chronicle in Part 5 of this book, it had to win that World Series in a way unlike any other team in the history of its sport had ever won one. That's how it had to be. Only in Philadelphia....

Little Moves, Big Dreams

PHILADELPHIA—There's no magic formula. There's no secret recipe. There's no runaway Amazon bestseller titled *How to Build a World Series Team or Your Money Back—All $200 Million of It.*"

But there are always lessons to be learned from the teams that make it to every World Series. And here is the lesson to be gleaned from the presence of the 2008 National League representative in the old Fall Classic, the Phillies: Don't forget the little moves.

The Phillies—as their loyal public has long noticed—are never that team that makes the Big Move. They don't sign the richest, most famous free agent on the market. They don't trade for the most seductive name on the July trading-deadline menu. Instead, they skulk along below the talk-show radar, looking for names that never make the lead story on *SportsCenter*, sometimes names that barely even dent the Transactions column.

Matt Stairs…Jayson Werth…Greg Dobbs.

Scott Eyre…J.C. Romero…Chad Durbin.

Those aren't players you build a team around. They're not the names you'll find on the grand World Series marquee. But add them to a cast of homegrown stars—to a Jimmy Rollins and a Chase Utley here, a Ryan Howard and a Cole Hamels there—and here's what those guys become: Players you win with.

Finding those kinds of players has been the house specialty of GM Pat Gillick for, oh, about three decades now. And 11 trips to the postseason later, with four different franchises, it's beginning to look as if he's on to something.

"You know, it's not always about that Big Free Agent," said Phillies pitcher Jamie Moyer, as his team was getting ready for a World Series while most of those Big Free Agents were getting ready to hit their favorite pitching wedge. "Sometimes, that Big Free Agent can create a problem."

You don't need us to start running down the list of all those Big Free Agents and the problems they've left in their wakes. You don't even need us to start running down the long list of teams that have reeled in those free agents and found out, once they'd rounded them all up, that their pieces still didn't fit.

They're obvious, but this story isn't about them. It's about a team and a general manager who paid extra-special attention to those smaller details—and to how those little moves helped glue their bigger pieces together.

That's the moral of the 2008 Phillies: Winning isn't always about dollars. And it isn't about July 31. And it isn't about making headlines on December 14. It's about finding pieces of all shapes and sizes—and then making them fit.

"And that," said assistant GM Mike Arbuckle, "is a credit to Pat, because I think he has great instincts and feel for what those smaller pieces can be to your club."

Unlike many people in this line of work, Gillick and his most trusted advisors—Arbuckle, Ruben Amaro Jr., Gordon Lakey, Charlie Kerfeld, and Chuck LaMar—have never gotten real stoked up about the stuff their fans and media hordes obsess on all off-season.

That doesn't mean we're all wrong when we pass along those 187,946 Johan Santana trade rumors in any given week in January. But what Gillick has spent his career demonstrating is that there are other ways to win.

"I know that's what people want to hear about," Arbuckle said. "People want to hear about a club going out and getting the Big Guy.... But if you can't get that big fish, what you have to do is try to take a sound baseball approach.

"And sometimes that sound baseball approach isn't what fans may want to hear at the time. Sometimes, that sound baseball approach may be a couple of smaller moves that supplement what you know you already have, and it's what you need to put you over the hump."

So at the July trading deadline, for example, Gillick balked at the asking price on a slew of left-handed relievers on the market. Exactly one week later, he was able to go out and deal for a left-handed reliever as good as any of them—Scott Eyre—from the Cubs for only a middle-range pitching prospect (Class A reliever Brian Schlitter).

Eyre, whom the Cubs had just designated for assignment, then made that trade look especially brilliant by compiling a 1.88 ERA in 19 appearance for the Phillies.

You might say that was luck. Except the year before, the Phillies swooped in and picked up their other left-handed bullpen piece, J.C. Romero, for just about nothing after the Red Sox had cut him loose.

All that move turned into was a guy who held left-handed hitters to a .104 batting average (14-for-138) over the next year and a half—after *getting released*.

Then there's the man who hit arguably the most important pinch home run in Phillies history—Stairs. He, too, was a player Gillick traded for in August after his old team (Toronto) had designated him for assignment. But he fit a need the Phillies had been looking to fill for weeks—a home-run threat off the bench. And one mammoth NLCS bomb off Jonathan Broxton later, that trade never looked better.

"He was a veteran guy who had played a lot of big games," Arbuckle said. "He has big power, and obviously our manager [Charlie Manuel] likes power. He was a guy we thought could do exactly what he did."

But this team was overstuffed with acquisitions of exactly this same ilk. Let's run through some more:

Dobbs: Claimed on waivers in January of 2007 when the Mariners were doing some roster maneuvering. A player Gillick had always liked since his days in Seattle. Over the next two seasons, Dobbs got more pinch hits (36) than any player in the National League but also started 123 games, most of them at third base.

Werth: Signed as a free agent, for $850,000, in December 2006, after the Dodgers non-tendered him. Gillick was the GM in Baltimore when Werth was the Orioles' first-round pick in 1997, then kept his eye on him throughout Werth's frustrating battles with wrist problems in 2005 and 2006. Werth then gradually worked himself into an every-day right-fielder and in 2008 hit more homers (24) than Justin Morneau or David Ortiz and had a higher slugging percentage (.498) than Magglio Ordonez or Carlos Pena.

Durbin: Non-tendered in 2007 by the Tigers because he was arbitration-eligible. Signed by the Phillies to a bargain free-agent deal (one year, $900,000). Became one of their most useful and versatile bullpen pieces (2.87 ERA in 71 appearances), despite running out of gas in September.

Moyer: Another August trade (in 2006), another trade for a player Gillick went way back with, to their days in Seattle. Moyer was 43 when the Phillies traded for him and was viewed by some folks as being close to the end of the trail. Well, apparently not. Over the next 26 months, he had exactly the same record (35–21) as Josh Beckett and Carlos Zambrano. In fact, only six pitchers in baseball had more wins than Moyer since that trade.

So let's review. Not one of the seven players we've mentioned here—Eyre, Romero, Stairs, Dobbs, Werth, Durbin, and Moyer—was a major free-agent signing. Two had been non-tendered by their old teams. One had been released. Two had been designated for assignment. Three were traded for *after* the trading deadline. One was a waiver claim.

The three signed as free agents cost barely more than $2 million *combined* at the time. The three they traded for cost them a total of four minor-leaguers, none of them top prospects.

The three hitters combined for 35 homers and a .283 average in 661 at-bats. The four pitchers went 28–15 with a 3.27 ERA and two saves in 357⅓ innings. The Phillies wouldn't have advanced this far without any of them.

And beyond what they've contributed on the stats sheet, they've all been popular clubhouse figures who added to the chemistry of one of the closest teams in baseball. But that's no accident, either.

"Pat's done a good job here," said Moyer, "because Pat really goes out and beats the pavement. It's not just going out and signing people just to sign them. I think he really looks into individuals. It's really easy to say, 'Hey, that guy's a good player.' But what about personality? Who is he? How can this person help this club, not only on the field but off the field? And Pat really works hard at that.

"Pat knows a lot of people. He's been around a long time, and he has a lot of experience. And that's one of the biggest intangible things he brings to this club. You don't see it written about a whole lot or talked about a whole lot in the media. But I've known Pat for a long time, and he's very observant. He does his homework. He goes the extra mile, and

I respect that. The teams that I've been on that he's been in charge of, we spend a lot of time together as players. And it's really enjoyable to be in a clubhouse with quality people, where there's not a barrier between players."

Pat Gillick turned 71 years old in August. He said before the 2008 season that this would be his last year as a general manager, and he picked an excellent year to pack up his office supplies. But his record continues to speak for itself. And when it does, it tells you there was obviously no baseball reason this man needed to retire.

Typically, when Pat Gillick was standing on the podium in Dodger Stadium for the presentation of the National League championship trophy, he deflected attention away from himself.

Even more typically, he heaped the credit on his predecessor, Ed Wade, for doing "a tremendous job getting the nucleus here." Because that nucleus preceded him, Gillick claimed, all he did was "kind of filled in around what Ed had in place."

But there's more to that filling-in than just throwing money at whoever will take it. And this team was living proof.

"I think Pat is a huge believer that a winning team is a sum of all the pieces," Arbuckle said. "And if you do it right, the sum of those pieces can turn out to be greater than all the individual pieces."

And it was the sum of these pieces that led the Phillies all the way to the World Series.

Why the Phillies Will Win the World Series

I wrote these words before Game 1 of the 2008 World Series. It's amazing I haven't since been hired by psychics.com.

The Philadelphia Phillies are going to win the World Series.

That is not a sentence many living citizens of this planet have ever typed before. But these are not your great-grandfather's Phillies.

These Phillies won't be playing in this World Series because they're the best team in the National League. They're here because they're the toughest team in the National League. And that toughness is the biggest reason I think they'll win.

"They're the most mentally tough team" in the field, an NL general manager told me three weeks ago. And he was just the lead singer in a chorus of GMs, scouts, coaching staffs, and players who have run into this team along the way. These people are always talking about "the way they play," and "how hard they play" and how much fun it is to watch these Phillies play. And remember, these are men who all work and play for *other teams.*

These Phillies don't seem imprisoned by their team's tortured past. In an odd way, they almost seem inspired by it. They constantly talk, right out loud, about how driven they are to write their own history, make their own mark, put their own stamp on their franchise and their ballpark. This is a group that sets the bar as high as it can be set, and a group of players who seem remarkably comfortable on this stage. And that's a quality that is going to show up throughout this World Series.

They've won 12 games this year in which they trailed after seven innings. They've won 29 games decided from the seventh inning on. They've won a half-dozen games they trailed by two runs or more in the eighth inning or later—including a defining NLCS game in Los Angeles. They never, ever feel they're out of a game. And that's another quality that is going to show up throughout this World Series.

They may not have the best starting rotation in this World Series, but they do have the best starting pitcher—Cole Hamels. I expect him to win Game 1, set the tone, and buy the offense a night to apply the Rustoleum after a week off. History does tell us that 10 of the last 11 Game 1 winners have gone on to win the Series. So Game 1 starters are often Series-changers. And Hamels fits that mold.

The Phillies also have the best bullpen and the best closer (Brad Lidge) in this World Series. And that's another quality all modern World Series winners share.

Much like the Rockies of 2007, this team heads into this World Series playing as well as it has ever played. Maybe 20–5 isn't 21–1, but it's the same stratosphere. The difference, though, is that these Phillies aren't just a good team that got hot. They're a team that was built to win, a team with all the ingredients to win, and *then* they got hot.

As the Rockies found out last October, it isn't always the hottest team that wins the World Series. But when the hottest team is also the toughest team, that's a whole different story.

So I'm writing a sentence that feels crazy just to tap out on my keyboard. But I'm writing it anyway: The Philadelphia Phillies are going to win the World Series. Phillies in six.

Birth of an October Legend

ST. PETERSBURG, FLORIDA—The names on the list are the names of men who have carved their legends in the month of October: Josh Beckett. Randy Johnson. Curt Schilling. Jack Morris. John Smoltz. Orel Hershiser.

We know their names because October was their kind of month. And they belong on that list because they once did something very few pitchers have ever done. They all won four starts in the same postseason. And now they have company.

The latest name to join them on that list is a 24-year-old left-hander named Cole Hamels. And with every time the Phillies handed him the baseball in October 2008, it became more apparent that he is one of this sport's most special talents.

He won Game 1 of the 2008 World Series, beating the Tampa Bay Rays, 3–2, in the Land of the Cowbells. It wouldn't be accurate to say he won that game for his team all by himself, but it *would* be accurate to say the Phillies won this game, in large part, because Cole Hamels just wasn't going to let them lose it.

"You just got the feeling he was not going to let anything happen to upset that game," said teammate Scott Eyre, after Hamels had finished spinning off seven innings of five-hit, two-run domination. "He was going to keep making pitches. And he was going to keep trying to get outs until they told him, 'You're done.'"

He was done, as it turned out, after 102 pitches. He was done because his manager, Charlie Manuel, thought it was time to unleash his unhittable late-inning bullpen tag team, Ryan Madson and Brad Lidge, for a devastating, six-up, six-down, three-strikeout grand finale in the eighth and ninth.

But this was Cole Hamels' show. And it became, officially, Cole Hamels' month, an October for the history books. So let's take a look at just some of the entries he had already made in those history books after his first four starts:

- He was 4–0, with a 1.55 ERA in those four starts, with 27 strikeouts in 29 innings. That made him only the 10th starting pitcher in history to win four games in one postseason, joining the six names above, plus Dave Stewart, David Wells, and Burt Hooton.
- And because he had another start looming in Game 5, he gave himself a chance to tie the all-time record for most wins in a single postseason, held by Randy Johnson (2001) and Francisco Rodriguez (2002). But all of K-Rod's wins that year, and one of Johnson's, came in relief. So Hamels was in position to become the first starting pitcher *ever* to win five times in one postseason.
- Hamels also became only the fourth pitcher ever to win Game 1 of an LDS, LCS, and World Series in a single postseason. The other three are Smoltz in 1996, Wells in 1998, and Beckett last year. But Hamels was the only member of that group who won three Game 1s *and* a series-clincher in one postseason (since he also won Game 5 of the NLCS).

Cole Hamels fires home against the Tampa Bay Rays in the first inning of Game 1 of the World Series on October 22, 2008.

- Finally, Hamels' Game 1 win made him the third-youngest left-handed starter in history to win a World Series opener. Only Babe Ruth and Ray Sadecki (both 23) were younger. And Hamels was the first left-hander to win a Game 1 on the road in 22 years—since Boston's Bruce Hurst beat the Mets in Shea Stadium in 1986.

So this fellow made it more clear, with every October journey to the mound, that he is baseball's most irreplaceable animal—a genuine, no-question-about-it No. 1 starter. And as his friend, teammate, and mentor, Jamie Moyer, put it, "It's great to be on a team that can rely on somebody like that."

Yeah, those aces can come in handy, all right. Especially at times like this. Because if you were going to draw up a formula for How to Win Game 1 of a World Series, "you wouldn't do it *that* way," laughed Jimmy Rollins after one of his team's strangest nights all season.

Yessir, if you're trying to win Game 1 of the World Series, we really don't advise you to do stuff like becoming the first team in history to go 0-for-13 with runners in scoring position in a World Series game.

And we really don't advise you to try to beat one of the hottest teams on earth on a night when your leadoff man (Rollins) and cleanup hitter (Howard) go a combined 0-for-9 with five strikeouts.

And we really, really don't advise you to try winning a game in which you leave 11 men on base, get another runner thrown out at the plate, and foul up two routine ground balls to the first baseman, all in the space of one crazy evening.

"But hey," Rollins chuckled, "it worked."

Yeah, it worked, all right. But the way it worked was so inexplicable that even the men in the middle of it got a little mixed up.

At one point after this game, for instance, Shane Victorino saw an ESPN graphic on the clubhouse TV that said his team had just gone 0-for-13 with runners in scoring position.

"Wait, we weren't 0-for-13 with runners in scoring position," he yelped.

Uh, yes, you were, his favorite gang of media inquisitors informed him.

"Oh, okay, we were," he said. "But I scored."

Right, he was informed. But he didn't score on a hit. He scored on a fourth-inning ground ball.

"Okay, we were 0-fer, but we still scored a damn run," Victorino retorted. "So take that 0-fer and shove it up…" (ehhh, no need to finish *this* sentence). "So we still manufactured a run. We don't have to get a hit to score a run. That's what I meant."

Sure. That's exactly what he meant. Just as soon as he finally figured out what he meant after he meant it. Or something like that.

But whatever he meant, "I'm sure tomorrow will be different," Rollins said. "I'm sure we can't go 0-for-13 with runners in scoring position *again* and win another game, 3–2. That's hard to do."

No kidding. But they did it. Somehow.

They did it because their irrepressible second baseman, Chase Utley, pounded a two-run homer off Rays starter Scott Kazmir in the first inning of the first World Series game of his life.

And they did it because, in Victorino's words, they "manufactured" an insurance run in the fourth on two singles and two ground-ball outs.

But mostly, they did it because the man on the mound, Cole Hamels, was fabulous.

He was arguably the best starting pitcher on either team in this World Series. But more than that, he was the most important starting pitcher on either team. And his teammates seemed well aware of exactly how important he really was.

"Our first thought," said Lidge afterward, "was, *We've got Cole Hamels on the mound. So we need to win.*"

And if that's the role his team wants to put him in, "He likes being in that position," said his pitching coach, Rich Dubee. "I think Cole's mentality is knowing that he's got stardom written all over him, and he thrives on that position."

So does that mean, Dubee was asked, that Hamels goes into games like this knowing he has to win?

"No," Dubee deadpanned. "He thinks he's going to go out and throw a no-hitter."

And on a night like this, facing hitters who have barely seen him, his teammates joke about just how possible that might be. When Cole Hamels unfurls the most untouchable change-up in baseball (or, at least, the most untouchable change-up thrown by anyone not named Johan Santana), it barely seems like a fair fight.

Asked if he ever feels sorry for hitters who have never seen that change-up before, Eyre replied, "Sometimes, because you know it's coming. When they get two strikes, we're all out there in the bullpen going, 'Here it comes.' And they swing right through it."

Oh, the Rays didn't swing through all of them, not on this night. Akinori Iwamura went 3-for-3 off Hamels, including a two-out, fifth-inning RBI double that narrowed the score to 3–2.

And Carl Crawford, a man who hadn't homered since June 27, hammered a solo homer off Hamels in the fourth.

And Hamels needed two B.J. Upton double-play balls—including a bases-loaded rocket to third base in the third inning—to wriggle out of two early jams.

But even though he's only 24, Cole Hamels always seems as if he's in total control—and not just of these career-defining baseball games, but of himself.

"He was walking around this afternoon like it was just another game," said Moyer. "I went out in the dugout early tonight before the game, and I sensed it even there. We had a conversation, and it was not like, 'Ho-hum, who cares.' It was, 'I'm ready to pitch. I've done all my prep work. And now I'm ready to go.' And he does it not with arrogance, not with cockiness. It's just confidence. It's just, 'I expect to go out and do it.'"

Hamels has talked often of wanting to be the guy on the mound in these games, in these moments. But even he said on this night that it hadn't hit him yet that this was the World Series.

"I think I'll still kind of play it slow and easy until the World Series is over," he said, "until I really get excited about it."

Well, if he really wanted to wait another week to figure out where he was and what he was doing, that was cool with his teammates—because they understood exactly what they were watching. They were watching greatness unfold before their eyes. And even better, they were watching it in the month that matters more than all the other months.

World Series, Game 1,
October 22, 2008, at Tampa
Phillies 3, Rays 2

Philadelphia	AB	R	H	RBI	BB	SO	LOB	AVG
Rollins, SS	5	0	0	0	0	2	5	.000
Werth, RF	4	1	2	0	1	1	0	.500
Utley, 2B	4	1	2	2	1	0	1	.500
Howard, 1B	4	0	0	0	1	3	4	.000
Burrell, LF	3	0	0	0	1	2	1	.000
1-Bruntlett, PR-LF	1	0	0	0	0	0	2	.000
Victorino, CF	4	1	2	0	0	1	4	.500
Feliz, 3B	3	0	2	0	1	0	0	.667
Coste, DH	4	0	0	0	0	0	5	.000
Ruiz, C	3	0	0	1	1	0	2	.000
Totals	35	3	8	3	6	9	24	

1-Ran for Burrell in the 7th.

BATTING
2B: Werth 2 (2, Kazmir, Balfour).
HR: Utley (1, 1st inning off Kazmir, 1 on, 1 out).
TB: Werth 4; Utley 5; Victorino 2; Feliz 2.
RBI: Utley 2 (2), Ruiz (1).
Runners left in scoring position, 2 out: Burrell; Rollins; Victorino 2; Bruntlett 2.
Team LOB: 11.

BASERUNNING
SB: Utley 2 (2, 2nd base off Wheeler/Navarro, 2nd base off Howell/Navarro), Werth (1, 3rd base off Wheeler/Navarro).

FIELDING
E: Howard (1, fielding).
DP: 2 (Feliz-Utley-Howard, Utley-Rollins-Howard).
Pickoffs: Hamels (Pena at 1st base).

Tampa Bay	AB	R	H	RBI	BB	SO	LOB	AVG
Iwamura, 2B	4	0	3	1	0	0	0	.750
Upton, CF	4	0	0	0	0	1	5	.000
Pena, 1B	4	0	0	0	0	1	0	.000
Longoria, 3B	4	0	0	0	0	3	0	.000
Crawford, LF	4	1	1	1	0	0	0	.250
Aybar, DH	3	0	0	0	0	1	0	.000
Navarro, C	3	0	0	0	0	2	0	.000
Zobrist, RF	3	0	1	0	0	0	0	.333
Bartlett, SS	1	1	0	0	2	0	0	.000
Totals	30	2	5	2	2	8	5	

BATTING
2B: Iwamura (1, Hamels).
HR: Crawford (1, 4th inning off Hamels, 0 on, 2 out).
TB: Iwamura 4; Crawford 4; Zobrist.
RBI: Crawford (1), Iwamura (1).
2-out RBI: Crawford; Iwamura.
Runners left in scoring position, 2 out: Upton.
GIDP: Upton 2.
Team LOB: 3.

BASERUNNING
SB: Bartlett (1, 2nd base off Hamels/Ruiz).
CS: Pena (1, 2nd base by Hamels/Ruiz).
PO: Pena (1st base by Hamels).

FIELDING
E: Pena (1, missed catch).
Outfield assists: Upton (Victorino at home).
DP: (Upton-Navarro).

Philadelphia	IP	H	R	ER	BB	SO	HR	ERA
Hamels (W, 1-0)	7.0	5	2	2	2	5	1	2.57
Madson (H, 1)	1.0	0	0	0	0	1	0	0.00
Lidge (S, 1)	1.0	0	0	0	0	2	0	0.00

Tampa Bay	IP	H	R	ER	BB	SO	HR	ERA
Kazmir (L, 0-1)	6.0	6	3	3	4	4	1	4.50
Howell	0.2	1	0	0	1	2	0	0.00
Balfour	1.2	1	0	0	1	2	0	0.00
Miller	0.1	0	0	0	0	1	0	0.00
Wheeler	0.1	0	0	0	0	0	0	0.00

WP: Howell; IBB: Utley (by Balfour); Pitches-strikes: Hamels 102-66, Madson 18-11, Lidge 15-11, Kazmir 110-73, Howell 19-11, Balfour 27-17, Miller 4-3, Wheeler 5-4; Groundouts-flyouts: Hamels 10-5, Madson 0-2, Lidge 0-1, Kazmir 5-8, Howell 0-0, Balfour 1-2, Miller 0-0, Wheeler 0-1; Batters faced: Hamels 26, Madson 3, Lidge 3, Kazmir 28, Howell 4, Balfour 7, Miller 1, Wheeler 1; Inherited runners-scored: Balfour 2-0, Miller 2-0, Wheeler 2-0; Umpires: HP: Tim Welke. 1B: Kerwin Danley. 2B: Fieldin Culbreth. 3B: Tom Hallion. LF: Jeff Kellogg. RF: Tim Tschida.

Weather: 72 degrees, dome; Wind: Indoors; T: 3:23; Att: 40,783.

Useless
Information

- My favorite Game 1 Useless Info tidbit was unearthed by the Elias Sports Bureau. Before Chase Utley, no player had hit a home run in the top of the first inning in Game 1 of any World Series in 42 years. Back in 1966, Frank Robinson homered in the top of the first, and Brook Robinson homered in the very next at-bat. Then no one did it after them for the next four decades.

- ESPN research genius Jason McCallum noticed that Utley was the first player in history whose last name starts with a U to homer in a World Series. That left only four letters still homerless—I, X, Q, and Z. But unfortunately, Akinori Iwamura and Ben Zobrist would fail in their quest to knock their favorite letters off the list in this Series.

- Oh. And one more thing. Utley was the first Phillie in history to hit a home run in his first World Series at-bat.

- How 'bout this funky list of Phillies starting pitchers who won Game 1 of a World Series: Grover Cleveland Alexander (1915), Bob Walk (1980), John Denny (1983), and Cole Hamels (2008).

- One more from the Elias Sports Bureau: Jimmy Rollins and Ryan Howard combined to go 0-for-9, with five strikeouts, in this game—and the Phillies *won*. In their five regular seasons as teammates, those two never had a game where they combined for zero hits and at least five whiffs in nine at-bats or more.

Game 2: October 23, 2008

Outs Are Good?

ST. PETERSBURG, FLORIDA—Someday, many decades from now, historians will look back on the first World Series victory in Tampa Bay Rays history.

And when they do, they will recall the events of Game 2, 2008, at Tropicana Field and, with voices trembling, they'll be able to sum up those events with one magic word: Huh?

We'd already learned, in the Rays' stunning ALCS triumph over the Red Sox, that this team could score runs with its legs (10 stolen bases). We's also learned that the Rays could score runs with their thunder (16 homers).

What we never learned is that the Rays also could score runs the way they scored them in Game 2, in the 4–2 win over the Phillies that evened the 2008 World Series at a win apiece: By making outs.

Really. You know, it's a funny thing. We'd be willing to bet that, before Game 2, we lived in a land of 300 million Americans who all believed, as one unified nation, that making outs was the one thing in baseball you would most want to avoid—with the possible exception of learning that Scott Boras was now representing your cleanup hitter.

But then along came this historic baseball event to teach us that we've had it all wrong—that we've had it all wrong since birth, in fact.

Outs are good. At least if they're the right kinds of outs. And in Game 2, the Rays made all the right outs. Or something like that.

"That's the cool thing about us," said Rays first baseman Carlos Pena, the resident voice of reason in this group. "We're multidimensional. Even when we're hitting the long ball, we're still thinking small. We're mature enough to understand that big things happen when you focus on the smallest of things."

And friends, things don't get much smaller in baseball than outs. So let's review how the Rays scored the four runs that changed this World Series, at least for one night:

- Ground ball to the shortstop.
- Another ground ball to the shortstop.
- A safety squeeze bunt built around a man who might have a tough time outrunning John Daly.
- And a hit that scored one run but got a second runner thrown out at the plate.

That, ladies and gentlemen, was the winning team's entire attack in a World Series game that they actually *won*.

It was all so thrilling, so electrifying, so downright inspirational that Rays manager Joe Maddon admitted he turned to his bench coach, Dave Martinez, and gushed, "This is what we have to emphasize next year in spring training—scoring runs with outs."

Yep, he really said that. And well he should, because it was that kind of night.

On one hand, that team the Rays were playing, the Phillies, continued to work harder to avoid scoring runs than any team in modern World Series history. The Phillies somehow went 1-for-28 with runners in scoring position over the first two games—the worst two-game RISP batting average (.036) by any World Series team in history.

But on the other hand, while all that clutch ineptitude was going on, it was the youngest juggernaut in baseball that went out and demonstrated that putting those runs on the board doesn't have to be as tough as the Phillies were making it look.

"We have to play small ball," said the Game 2–winning pitcher, James Shields. "It's the World Series. That's the way you play the game. That's the way you win championships."

Now, to be honest, as the Rays proved in the ALCS, there are other ways. But doing whatever it takes—*that's* what wins championships.

And if the ultimate definition of "whatever it takes" consists of "flashing the squeeze sign *twice*, even with Cliff Floyd on third base," then it's now official. The Rays will, clearly, do *anything* to score a run.

Because that's what they did with a 3–0 lead in the fourth inning of this game, much to the shock of even their own troops.

"To be honest," said Pena, "when I saw that sign, I said, 'Oh, Lord.'"

So why would he have felt a need to speak to powers higher even than Joe Maddon about a move like this? Well, for one thing, this team didn't execute a single successful squeeze bunt all season. And, for another thing, Floyd was the runner on third base. And let's just say nobody has mistaken him lately for Asafa Powell.

"Hey, I'm slow," Floyd said, at his earnest best. "Let's get that straight."

"I don't want to say he's as slow as a turtle," said Shields, "because he did steal a bag this year. It'll probably be the last stolen base of his career, but he did steal one."

So any manager who was willing to give Cliff Floyd the green light to steal a base would, obviously, be a manager with no fear of giving Jason Bartlett the squeeze sign with Floyd at third base.

In fact, Maddon was so willing to give that sign, he even gave it twice.

And because that happened, in real life, in a jam-packed ballpark in the middle of the night, this World Series had just taken a dramatic, pivotal turn.

The Phillies suddenly led this Series two games to one. They led it even though they were hitting .061 (2-for-33) with runners in scoring position. They led it even though neither of those two hits left the infield, and one of them didn't even score a run.

They led it even though their late-inning defensive replacement had produced more runs than their leadoff hitter. And they led it even though they'd allowed that team they were playing to score eight consecutive runs, over two games, on plays that included either an out or an error.

"It's a funny game," said Phillies manager Charlie Manuel when this insanity was over. "That's how the game goes."

Well, it's not supposed to go quite like this. Is it? But somehow or other, the Phillies found themselves two games away from winning the World Series and in prime position to finish that job. Of the previous 51 World Series that were tied at 1–1, the winner of Game 3 went on to win the Series two-thirds of the time.

But one thing none of those other World Series featured was a game that didn't start until after 10:00 PM, as this one did. You can thank the weather front from hell for making that possible.

And that set the stage for a long night's journey into day that eventually led us to an unprecedented burst of 1:00 AM craziness, starring the two Phillies everybody expected to take over a crucial World Series game—Eric Bruntlett and Carlos Ruiz.

It was Bruntlett, a utility infielder who unexpectedly spent most of this season serving as Pat Burrell's late-inning defensive caddy in left field, who would wind up scoring the winning run in this game—at 1:47 AM.

Asked if he could recall the last time he'd scored a run at 1:47 AM, Bruntlett scratched his head and concluded, "I'm pretty sure that's a first for me."

And the way he came to score that winning run? That had to be a first, too.

His journey started with—what else?—a J.P. Howell fastball that plunked him in the thigh with nobody out in the ninth. And that was about the most *normal* thing that happened in this inning.

Before you knew it, the Rays were unfurling their first World Series double-switch in franchise history. And reliever Grant Balfour was skipping a wild pitch to the backstop.

And that wild pitch then caromed back to catcher Dioner Navarro so fast that he decided to try to nail Bruntlett at second. But instead, Navarro sailed his throw into center field, sending Bruntlett to third.

And then Rays managerial innovator Joe Maddon was signaling for everybody's favorite 1:00 AM brainstorm—the old five-man infield. And that left the infield so overcrowded with Rays fielders that Phillies first baseman Ryan Howard quipped, "I thought they were about to send them all in on a blitz."

But the man who walked up to the plate after Maddon had ordered two intentional walks to load the bases said he wasn't looking out for any linebackers. He wasn't even sure how many infielders there were.

"I didn't know," said Carlos Ruiz. "I didn't count them."

It had already been quite the eventful evening for Ruiz, a .219 hitter who had turned into the Phillies' hottest October bat. The good news was, he'd hit a second-inning home run to put the Phillies ahead, 2–1. The bad news was, he'd also committed a crushing throwing error that allowed the Rays to tie the game in the eighth inning.

But he was about to have a moment that would make all his other moments disappear.

The ageless Jamie Moyer releases a pitch in Game 3 of the World Series on October 25, 2008.

The count got to 2-and-2. Towels swirled in the night. Nearly 46,000 exhausted voices did their best to wake up the residents of South Philadelphia. Balfour reared back and did what he does best—launch one more 95-mile-an-hour smokeball. And Carlos Ruiz took his mightiest swing, only to thunk a little hip-hopper down the third-base line that was about to turn the World Series upside down.

In raced Tampa Bay's brilliant third baseman, Evan Longoria. ("About the last thing you wanted in that situation was a ground ball," said the Phillies' Chris Coste. "And about the last person you'd want to field it was probably Longoria.")

Down the line sprinted Eric Bruntlett, heart pounding like a bass drum.

"It was one of those deals," Bruntlett said, "where it kind of feels like everything is in slow motion. You feel like you should be moving faster,

177

just because you want to get there so quick. So it felt like a long 90 feet. That's all I know."

Meanwhile, there was Ruiz, a man who doesn't exactly specialize in game-winning infield hits, let alone infield hits of any kind, pumping down the first-base line, listening for the sound that would tell him whether he'd just become an October hero.

"Then," Ruiz said, "I heard them cheering. And that's when I knew, 'Okay, it's over.'"

Longoria had just an instant to decide: Was this ball going foul or staying fair? Pick it up or let it go? Make a play or pray for luck?

He made the right call, but it was too late. He scrambled, bare-handed it, flipped it toward home—and eight feet over Navarro's head. Bedlam reigned. This game was over. The clock in center field said 1:47 AM.

"I was excited," said Carlos Ruiz, a man hitting .500 (4-for-8) in this World Series, "no matter what kind of hit it was. I said when I hit it, 'I'll take it. I'll take a win.'"

And this wasn't just any old win. It was a win that almost had turned into a disaster.

Three Phillies homers—by Ruiz, Chase Utley, and Ryan Howard—had lifted the Phillies to a 4–1 lead heading into the seventh. So this game should have been over, because when the Phillies led this big this late, they always won. After all, they'd gone 60–1 in games they led by three runs or more in the seventh inning or later.

And then it happened.

Jamie Moyer, 45 years and 342 days old, was nine outs away from becoming the oldest pitcher ever to win a World Series game or any kind of postseason game. Until the first hitter of the seventh inning, Carl Crawford, laid down a clinic of a drag bunt down the first-base line.

We'll never know quite how Moyer even got there, but he did. He lunged. He scooped up the baseball with his glove and flipped it to first in one spectacular motion.

"The way he got over there," laughed Howard later, "it was ninja-esque."

The baseball floated toward first. Howard snatched it out of the air with his bare hand. An instant later, Crawford's foot hit the bag.

And then, stunningly, first-base umpire Tom Hallion flashed the safe sign.

The groans that poured out of the seats made it feel like a Bartman Moment—Philadelphia style.

In a town that had gone titleless for 25 years, for a franchise that had won just one World Series, this had "ugly omen" written all over it. Especially when the Rays transformed it into a two-run inning that made it a 4–3 game. And even more so an inning later, when B.J. Upton willed himself to the game-tying run—with an infield single, a steal of second, a steal of third, and Ruiz's throwing error.

Had this game turned into a come-from-ahead loss, said Jimmy Rollins afterward, this would have been the call Philadelphians mourned for centuries.

"Oh yeah," Rollins said. "If we'd have lost, you know they'd have been talking about this one. That's when all the good conspiracy theories come out."

But you can toss that script into the old dumpster—because Carlos Ruiz's dribbler heard round the Delaware Valley made it all moot.

"That's a moment I'll remember the rest of my life," said the author of the first walk-off infield hit in World Series history. "I hope I can do it again tomorrow."

Okay, so it was actually today by then. But you never correct a hero—especially at 1:47 AM.

World Series, Game 3,
October 25, 2008, at Philadelphia
Phillies 5, Rays 4

Tampa Bay	AB	R	H	RBI	BB	SO	LOB	AVG
Iwamura, 2B	4	0	0	0	0	2	1	.273
Upton, CF	4	1	2	0	0	1	0	.333
Pena, 1B	3	0	0	1	2	2	.000
Longoria, 3B	4	0	0	0	2	2	.000
Crawford, LF	4	2	2	0	0	0	.250
Navarro, C	4	1	2	0	0	1	1	.400
Gross, RF	3	0	0	2	0	0	2	.000
Balfour, P	0	0	0	0	0	0	0	.000
Bartlett, SS	4	0	0	1	0	0	1	.286
Garza, P	2	0	0	0	0	0	1	.000
a-Aybar, PH	0	0	0	0	1	0	0	.000
Bradford, P	0	0	0	0	0	0	0	.000
Howell, P	0	0	0	0	0	0	0	.000
Zobrist, RF	0	0	0	0	0	0	0	.333
Totals	32	4	6	3	2	8	10	

a-Walked for Garza in the 7th.

BATTING
2B: Crawford (1, Moyer), Navarro (1, Moyer).
TB: Upton 2; Crawford 3; Navarro 3.
RBI: Gross 2 (2), Bartlett (2).
Runners left in scoring position, 2 out: Longoria.
SF: Gross.
Team LOB: 4.

BASERUNNING
SB: Upton 3 (3, 2nd base off Moyer/Ruiz, 2nd base off Madson/Ruiz, 3rd base off Madson/Ruiz), Crawford (1, 3rd base off Moyer/Ruiz).

FIELDING
E: Navarro (1, throw).
Pickoffs: Howell (Werth at 2nd base).

Philadelphia	AB	R	H	RBI	BB	SO	LOB	AVG
Rollins, SS	4	1	2	0	0	0	1	.143
Werth, RF	2	0	1	0	2	0	1	.364
Utley, 2B	4	1	1	2	0	1	3	.250
Howard, 1B	4	1	1	1	0	2	2	.231
Burrell, LF	3	0	0	0	0	2	1	.000
Bruntlett, LF	0	1	0	0	0	0	0	.500
Victorino, CF	3	0	0	0	1	1	0	.364
Feliz, 3B	3	0	0	0	0	2	0	.200
b-Dobbs, PH	0	0	0	0	1	0	0	.333
Ruiz, C	3	1	2	2	1	0	0	.500
Moyer, P	2	0	0	0	0	1	1	.000
Durbin, C, P	0	0	0	0	0	0	0	.000
Eyre, P	0	0	0	0	0	0	0	.000
a-Jenkins, PH	1	0	0	0	0	0	0	.000
Madson, P	0	0	0	0	0	0	0	.000
Romero, P	0	0	0	0	0	0	0	.000
Totals	29	5	7	5	5	9	9	

a-Grounded out for Eyre in the 7th. b-Intentionally walked for Feliz in the 9th.

BATTING
HR: Ruiz (1, 2nd inning off Garza, 0 on, 2 out), Utley (2, 6th inning off Garza, 0 on, 0 out), Howard (1, 6th inning off Garza, 0 on, 0 out).
TB: Rollins 2; Werth; Utley 4; Howard 4; Ruiz 5.
RBI: Utley 2 (4), Ruiz 2 (3), Howard (1).
2-out RBI: Ruiz.
Runners left in scoring position, 2 out: Burrell.
Team LOB: 6.

BASERUNNING
SB: Werth (2, 2nd base off Howell/Navarro).
CS: Rollins (1, 2nd base by Garza/Navarro).
PO: Werth (2nd base by Howell).

FIELDING
E: Ruiz (2, throw).

Tampa Bay	IP	H	R	ER	BB	SO	HR	ERA
Garza	6.0	6	4	4	2	7	3	6.00
Bradford	1.0	0	0	0	1	0	0	0.00
Howell (L, 0-1)	1.0	0	1	1	0	2	0	5.40
Balfour	0.0	1	0	0	2	0	0	0.00

Philadelphia	IP	H	R	ER	BB	SO	HR	ERA
Moyer	6.1	5	3	3	1	5	0	4.26
Durbin, C (H, 1)	0.1	0	0	0	1	0	0	0.00
Eyre (H, 1)	0.1	0	0	0	0	1	0	0.00
Madson (BS, 1)	0.2	1	1	1	0	1	0	5.40
Romero (W, 1-0)	1.1	0	0	0	0	1	0	0.00

Bradford pitched to 1 batter in the 8th; Howell pitched to 1 batter in the 9th; Balfour pitched to 3 batters in the 9th.

WP: Garza, Balfour; IBB: Victorino (by Balfour), Dobbs (by Balfour); HBP: Bruntlett (by Howell); Pitches-strikes: Garza 102-65, Bradford 15-8, Howell 16-8, Balfour 15-5, Moyer 96-64, Durbin, C 6-2, Eyre 6-3, Madson 15-7, Romero 15-10; Groundouts-flyouts: Garza 4-6, Bradford 2-1, Howell 0-0, Balfour 0-0, Moyer 4-10, Durbin, C 1-0, Eyre 0-0, Madson 1-0, Romero 2-1; Batters faced: Garza 25, Bradford 4, Howell 3, Balfour 3, Moyer 25, Durbin, C 2, Eyre 1, Madson 3, Romero 4; Inherited runners-scored: Howell 1-0, Balfour 1-1, Durbin, C 1-1, Eyre 1-0; Umpires: HP: Fieldin Culbreth. 1B: Tom Hallion. 2B: Jeff Kellogg. 3B: Tim Tschida. LF: Tim Welke. RF: Kerwin Danley.

Weather: 55 degrees, cloudy; Wind: 10 mph, L to R; T: 3:41 (1:31 delay); Att: 45,900.

Useless
Information

- When the Rays played their fabled five-man infield in the ninth inning, it was believed to be the first five-man infield in World Series history. And the manager who ordered it, Joe Maddon, is the same guy who once played a four-man *outfield* in the Rays' previous visit to Philadelphia, in 2006.

- A 45-year-old pitcher (Jamie Moyer) started this game for the Phillies. A 24-year-old pitcher (Matt Garza) started it for the Rays. That age difference—21 years, 8 days—was the largest between any two starting pitchers in World Series history.

- The Phillies hit three home runs off Garza in this game. Guess how many times he allowed three homers in a game during the regular season? None, of course.

- In 1975 Carlton Fisk hit one of the most famous game-ending home runs in World Series history. Between Fisk's hit and Carlos Ruiz's game-winning squibber in this game, only one other catcher had a walkoff World Series hit—the Reds' Joe Oliver, in 1990.

- Finally, is baseball a bizarre sport, or what? In Game 2, the Rays became the first World Series team since the 1923 Giants to score two runs in one inning on ground-ball outs. In Game 3, the Rays became the first team to do that in, oh, about 48 hours.

Game 4: October 26, 2008

One Win Away

PHILADELPHIA—They stood there in the ninth inning—all 45,903 of them. They spun their rally towels in the October night. They shredded what was left of their vocal cords. They counted down the outs.

Many of these red-shirted souls had waited a generation for this moment to come around again, just once. Many more had spent their whole lives wondering what it would feel like.

One win away.

In Philadelphia, nothing is ever certain. Nothing ever feels safe. Not when your team is the losingest franchise in the history of pro sports. Not when its fabled collapses were far more legendary than its one moment of triumph.

But in Citizens Bank Park, on this perfect autumn evening, all those usual fears, all that traditional dread, seemed to dissolve into the euphoria of a night millions of Philadelphians were almost completely unfamiliar with.

One win away.

The Phillies hung a 10–2 whomping on that team from Tampa Bay in Game 4 of a World Series that would redefine the psyche of an entire city. So the Phillies now led this Series three games to one, with their ace,

Cole Hamels, about to head for the mound in Game 5 with a chance to seal this deal.

If they were in the script-writing business, this was the script they would have written for themselves—handing the baseball to a guy who had already won four games this October, with a chance to win the World Series in the place they'd most like to win it.

In this town. Their town. A town that no longer looked at them and wondered how they would break all those millions of hearts. Again.

"I went out to throw a bullpen today," said pitcher Brett Myers, a man who had dreamed of this night for seven seasons. "And I heard one of the greatest things I've heard in a long time.

"It's 4:15 in the afternoon. The Eagles are playing across the street. There's two minutes left. And I'm hearing Phillies chants. And that's weird, man. I'm used to hearing Eagles chants all these years. So to hear that, it gave me chills. It told me, 'These people are ready to go.'"

Yeah, they couldn't have been more ready, in fact. Not after waiting 28 years for their baseball team to get back into this position. Not after waiting 25 years for *any* of their stinking teams, in any sport, to get back into this position.

So the love poured out of every corner of this ballpark. In Philadelphia, of all places. What a concept.

But you don't have to look too far over your shoulder to remember it hasn't always been a lovefest between this team and this town. These players have heard many, many sounds come wafting out of these seats over the years. And they sure weren't the same sounds they heard through their magical October.

So when they looked into the faces of the people in those seats, they were astonished by what they saw.

"It's awesome," said third baseman Greg Dobbs. "You can see the excitement, the intensity, the passion, the anticipation. You can see the sheer joy on people's faces. It's a great thing to see."

Then again, these people hadn't seen their baseball team lose for a long, long time. Since September 24, to be exact—a 10–4 regular-season loss to Atlanta.

Since then, the Phillies had won nine home games in a row. The first three of those wins, against Washington, clinched the NL East in the final weekend of the season. The next six came in October, against the Brewers, Dodgers, and Rays.

A win in Game 5 would make the Phillies the first team since the '99 Yankees to win a World Series while going undefeated in their home park in the postseason.

But one win away wasn't the same thing as no wins away. And there wasn't a voice in that locker room after Game 4 that didn't make sure to point that out.

"I've been here before, one win away," said reliever Scott Eyre, a member of a 2002 Giants team that lost Games 6 and 7 to the Angels. "And I really don't want to experience what happened then."

"I'm trying not to look too far ahead," said Myers, "because that's a good team we're playing. That team is very capable of winning three straight. They won 97 games this year.... So yeah, it's exciting. But at the same time, I'm trying to control the excitement, because we still have a job to do. It's not over yet."

Nevertheless, every night something seemed to happen to this team that had no logical business happening. You would have thought the Phillies couldn't possibly top winning Game 1 while going 0-for-13 with men in scoring position. Then you would have thought they couldn't possibly do anything stranger than winning Game 3 on a 60-foot dribbler at 13 minutes before 2:00 AM. But they might just have

Ryan Howard watches his three-run home run off of the Rays' Andy Sonnanstine in the fourth inning of Game 4 of the World Series on October 26, 2008.

pulled off the all-timer in Game 4. A home run by Joltin' Joe Blanton? In a World Series game? C'mon. Who wrote this screenplay? Will Ferrell?

"I just close my eyes and swing hard in case I make contact," said Game 4's unlikely home-run hero. "That's really the only thing I can say."

And when, he was asked, did he think it was safe to open those eyes again?

"I think when I went out and had to throw the next warm-up pitch in the next inning," Blanton said.

Howard's Homers

I can't decide. Did Ryan Howard have the greatest year any 199-strikeout whiff machine ever had? Or did he have the roughest year any 48-homer whomper ever had? Hey, you've got me. You figure it out.

On one hand, he almost won the National League MVP award. On the other, he didn't even win his own team's MVP award (Brad Lidge did).

The guy did get his batting average up to .251, which is pretty astounding for a fellow who was hitting .163 in May. But his missing average, thanks to those 199 strikeouts, computed to .326.

When Howard actually made contact, he had a higher batting average than Ichiro Suzuki (.372–.343). But he was so proficient at avoiding contact, he wound up with the lowest batting average in history (by nearly 30 points!) by a man who drove in 146 runs.

So how did this guy knock in those 146 runs? Well, it wasn't just because he hit so many baseballs that landed in somebody's popcorn box.

When there were runners on base, he was Joe DiMaggio. When there was nobody on base, he was Joe DePastino. Average with men on: .309. Average with nobody on: .196. That's an insane 103-point difference. What's up with that?

Trying to explain that ride on the roller-coaster isn't exactly Ryan Howard's favorite hobby, by the way. This is a man who, if given a choice between gall-bladder surgery and breaking down his swing, might very well say, "Which way's the O.R.?" But he will confess to this: He's human.

"I'm mortal," he said. "I bleed, just like everybody else bleeds. But it's just one of those things. That's the entire game. Everybody goes through hot streaks and cool streaks. And it's just making the adjustments to be able to get out of them."

Well, he made them. Finally. And it's a good thing for his team, because the Phillies never could have won without him.

In the final days of August, Howard finally stopped lunging, plunging, and hacking at every pitcher's pitch between the inside corner and Bala Cynwyd. And once he relaxed, started swinging at actual strikes, and noticed that left field was still out there in fair territory—right where he'd left it in 2006—he was a game-changer waiting to happen every at-bat.

From August 30 on, he hit .367, slugged .857, and led the solar system in home runs (12), RBIs (34), and runs scored (29). Of his final 36 hits, 22 were for extra bases. He even went 17 for his last 43 (.395) against left-handers.

And once he took off, the Phillies were happy to pile into his main cabin and let him fly them directly toward October.

"When he gets going," said Lidge, "we can start putting a thumping on people."

As you might have heard, it took Howard 12 postseason games to put a thumping on his first October home run. But once he got that first one out of the way, he mashed three homers and a single in a span of six World Series at-bats.

The Phillies never lost again, incidentally. And that, friends, is what's known in the baseball business as a related development.

All right, let's try to assess what exactly happened here. No pitcher—AL or NL—had launched a home run in a World Series game in 34 years, since Oakland's Ken Holtzman got to unfurl his trot in 1974. Since then, those sweet-swinging pitchers marching toward home plate had gone a scenic 40-for-424—which computes to a batting average of .094 if you're calculating along at your cubicle.

Meanwhile, no National League pitcher had hit a World Series homer in four decades—since Bob Gibson did it way back in 1968. So you had to figure that was going to change one of these Octobers.

But c'mon. Joe Blanton? A guy with two hits in his whole career (in 33 at-bats)? A guy with no home runs at any professional level? A guy who had never even swatted an extra-base hit?

How'd that happen?

"You know, I told him after his first couple of at-bats that he was trying to hit the deep ball," Blanton's buddy, Myers, deadpanned. "So I told him, 'Just try to stay short and sweet, like you do in BP. Try to go back up the middle.' Well, I don't think I got through to him."

Yeah, that's safe to say.

Blanton's thunderous fifth-inning hack was about as short and sweet as an 18-wheeler. Rays reliever Edwin Jackson fed him a 93-mile-per-hour flameball. And Blanton rocked the house with a massive shot over the flower pots in left-center, as his ballpark shook and his many admirers in uniform just about keeled over.

Uh, wait. Cancel that "almost."

"I fell off my chair in the bullpen," said reliever Clay Condrey. "I mean it. I fell right off my chair."

There are moments in the life of every team that make its players wonder if something is going on that is bigger than themselves. There are always things that happen to teams on this kind of roll that feel as if it's all meant to be.

"You know, I'm beginning to think," said Eyre, "that that was one of those things—a special thing that shouldn't have happened, that did."

Oh, a lot of other stuff happened in this game, we should probably add. And most of it was, to be honest, more important stuff than Joe Blanton's homer.

There were two Ryan Howard homers, for one thing—including a three-run opposite-field mash in the fourth inning that busted open what had been a tense 2–1 game. Those homers made Howard the first player in history to hit two home runs in a World Series game the same year in which he led the major leagues in homers.

There was also a fourth Phillies homer, by Jayson Werth in the eighth. And that made the Phillies the first team ever to hit four home runs in the same World Series game off four different pitchers.

And there was the other half of Joe Blanton's act—the half in which he did his day job, his mound job, about as well as it could be done.

He got them all the way to the seventh inning, as all four Phillies starters had done in this World Series, allowing only four hits and two runs. And his seven strikeouts were the fourth-most in history by a pitcher who also hit a World Series homer.

It was almost enough to make you forget that back in July, when the Phillies traded for Joe Blanton, he was viewed by the populace as the not-so-glamorous bargain-bin alternative to the pitchers his new town really wanted—CC Sabathia and Rich Harden. But the guy from the bargain bin is looking a lot better these days.

The Phillies went 12–4 in games he started, including seven wins in a row. He went 2–0 in October with a 3.18 ERA. And in Game 4 Blanton became just the second pitcher in the last 31 years to get traded in midseason and win a World Series game. (The other was Jeff Weaver, for the 2006 Cardinals.)

"He did exactly what we needed him to do," said Myers. "He was awesome tonight."

What they needed him to do, of course, was get them to the place they would find themselves in for Game 5: One win away.

Myers actually choked up with emotion after Game 4 as he thought about what his ballpark might look like and feel like with that title so close.

Howard contemplated what loomed just over that horizon and predicted, "This could be the craziest city in the world."

"I think it will be absolutely nuts," said Dobbs. "I think this city could explode the top right off. So you might want to hide. I don't want you to get crushed—because then, who would write the story?"

Well, how about the man across his own locker room—the one Phillie old enough to remember what a World Series parade looked like, the one Phillie who grew up right down the road and actually attended that World Series parade in 1980: Jamie Moyer.

"You know," Moyer said, "I think maybe because it took so long, there's a greater appreciation if it does happen. Sometimes, the longer you wait for things, the more you appreciate them."

How true. So it would be fascinating for all of them to see what was about to unfold in Citizens Bank Park in Game 5, on a night that millions of Philadelphians had awaited for what felt like 98 centuries. Because now they were here. Finally. One win away.

World Series, Game 4,
October 26, 2008, at Philadelphia
Phillies 10, Rays 2

Tampa Bay	AB	R	H	RBI	BB	SO	LOB	AVG
Iwamura, 2B	4	0	0	0	0	0	3	.200
Upton, CF	4	0	0	0	0	2	3	.250
Pena, 1B	3	0	0	0	1	2	0	.000
Longoria, 3B	4	0	0	0	0	3	1	.000
Crawford, LF	3	1	1	1	0	1	0	.267
Navarro, C	4	0	1	0	0	1	2	.357
Zobrist, RF	3	0	0	0	1	0	2	.167
Bartlett, SS	4	0	0	0	0	2	2	.182
Sonnanstine, P	1	0	1	0	0	0	0	1.000
a-Hinske, PH	1	1	1	1	0	0	0	1.000
Jackson, P	0	0	0	0	0	0	0	.000
b-Aybar, PH	1	0	1	0	0	0	0	.250
Wheeler, P	0	0	0	0	0	0	0	.000
Miller, P	0	0	0	0	0	0	0	.000
c-Baldelli, PH	1	0	0	0	0	1	1	.000
Totals	33	2	5	2	2	12	14	

Philadelphia	AB	R	H	RBI	BB	SO	LOB	AVG
Rollins, SS	5	3	3	0	0	0	0	.263
Werth, RF	4	2	2	2	1	0	2	.400
Utley, 2B	3	2	0	0	2	2	3	.200
Howard, 1B	4	2	3	5	1	0	2	.353
Burrell, LF	3	0	0	1	1	0	4	.000
Bruntlett, LF	1	0	0	0	0	0	0	.333
Victorino, CF	5	0	0	0	0	0	5	.250
Feliz, 3B	4	0	2	1	0	0	3	.286
Ruiz, C	4	0	1	0	0	0	1	.417
Blanton, P	3	1	1	1	0	1	3	.333
Durbin, C, P	0	0	0	0	0	0	0	.000
Eyre, P	0	0	0	0	0	0	0	.000
Madson, P	0	0	0	0	0	0	0	.000
a-Stairs, PH	1	0	0	0	0	1	0	.000
Romero, P	0	0	0	0	0	0	0	.000
Totals	37	10	12	10	5	4	23	

a-Homered for Sonnanstine in the 5th. b-Singled for Jackson in the 7th. c-Struck out for Miller in the 9th.

a-Struck out for Madson in the 8th.

BATTING
HR: Crawford (2, 4th inning off Blanton, 0 on, 2 out), Hinske (1, 5th inning off Blanton, 0 on, 2 out).
TB: Crawford 4; Navarro; Sonnanstine; Hinske 4; Aybar.
RBI: Crawford (2), Hinske (1).
2-out RBI: Crawford; Hinske.
Runners left in scoring position, 2 out: Navarro; Upton.
Team LOB: 7.

FIELDING
E: Iwamura 2 (2, fielding, fielding).
DP: 2 (Bartlett-Iwamura-Pena, Iwamura-Pena).

BATTING
2B: Rollins 2 (2, Sonnanstine, Wheeler), Werth (3, Jackson).
HR: Howard 2 (3, 4th inning off Sonnanstine, 2 on, 1 out; 8th inning off Miller, 1 on, 1 out), Blanton (1, 5th inning off Jackson, 0 on, 2 out), Werth (1, 8th inning off Wheeler, 1 on, 1 out).
TB: Rollins 5; Werth 6; Howard 9; Feliz 2; Ruiz; Blanton 4.
RBI: Burrell (1), Feliz (1), Howard 5 (6), Blanton (1), Werth 2 (2).
2-out RBI: Feliz; Blanton.
Runners left in scoring position, 2 out: Feliz 2; Blanton 2.
GIDP: Burrell.
Team LOB: 8.

FIELDING
E: Romero (1, throw).

Tampa Bay	IP	H	R	ER	BB	SO	HR	ERA
Sonnanstine (L, 0-1)	4.0	6	5	3	3	2	1	6.75
Jackson	2.0	2	1	1	1	1	1	4.50
Wheeler	1.1	3	2	2	0	1	1	6.75
Miller	0.2	1	2	2	1	0	1	18.00

Philadelphia	IP	H	R	ER	BB	SO	HR	ERA
Blanton (W, 1-0)	6.0	4	2	2	2	7	2	3.00
Durbin, C	0.1	1	0	0	0	0	0	0.00
Eyre (H, 2)	0.1	0	0	0	0	0	0	0.00
Madson (H, 2)	1.1	0	0	0	0	3	0	3.00
Romero	1.0	0	0	0	0	2	0	0.00

Blanton pitched to 1 batter in the 7th.

IBB: Howard (by Jackson); HBP: Crawford (by Blanton); Pitches-strikes: Sonnanstine 89-52, Jackson 32-19, Wheeler 22-16, Miller 10-4, Blanton 99-61, Durbin, C 5-4, Eyre 5-2, Madson 16-11, Romero 19-11; Groundouts-flyouts: Sonnanstine 1-9, Jackson 4-1, Wheeler 0-2, Miller 1-1, Blanton 6-5, Durbin, C 0-1, Eyre 0-1, Madson 1-0, Romero 1-0; Batters faced: Sonnanstine 24, Jackson 8, Wheeler 6, Miller 4, Blanton 25, Durbin, C 2, Eyre 1, Madson 4, Romero 4; Inherited runners-scored: Durbin, C 1-0, Eyre 2-0, Madson 2-0; Umpires: HP: Tom Hallion. 1B: Jeff Kellogg. 2B: Tim Tschida. 3B: Tim Welke. LF: Kerwin Danley. RF: Fieldin Culbreth.

Weather: 54 degrees, overcast; Wind: 7 mph, Out to CF; T: 3:08; Att: 45,903.

Useless
Information

- Only two National League pitchers in the last 50 years have hit a World Series home run—Joe Blanton and Bob Gibson. Blanton owned two career hits and a spectacular .061 lifetime batting average at the time of his homer. When Gibson went deep in 1968, on the other hand, he was the proud owner of 143 career hits and a batting average (.194) more than three times as hefty as Blanton's.

- Before Blanton's home run, he'd never even gotten an extra-base hit at any point in his big-league career. So this homer, according to the Elias Sports Bureau, made him the first player in the history of the sport whose first extra-base hit was a World Series home run.

- Ryan Howard finally awakened with two home runs in this game. He became the first player ever to lead the major leagues in homers and have a multi-homer World Series game in the same season, according to Elias.

- It's amazing all the stuff that happened in this World Series that didn't happen all season. Here's another: Andy Sonnanstine walked Pat Burrell with the bases loaded to force in the Phillies' first run. So how many times has Sonnanstine ever walked in a run in his career? Never, of course. In 54 starts.

- Guess how many World Series at-bats with runners in scoring position it took for the Phillies to finally get a hit that made it to the outfield. Would you believe 40? They were 2-for-29, with two infield singles, before Pedro Feliz actually lined an RBI single to left in the third inning.

Rain-Delay Theater

PHILADELPHIA—The Phillies came to the ballpark for Game 5 thinking they were about to hand the World Series over to Mr. October, Cole Hamels.

Little did they know they were about to hand it over to Bud Selig's favorite Doppler 10,000.

And because they did, this World Series was never going to be the same. You understand that, right?

It was no longer going to be known for Carlos Ruiz's 2:00 AM walk-off squibber or Joe Blanton's Babe Ruth impression or Cliff Floyd's mad dash home on the most improbable squeeze bunt of modern times.

Nope.

This one was now going down in a whole different chapter of World Series lore: Weather lore.

We can figure out exactly where it fits into the grand history of baseball meteorology one of these years. But in the meantime, all anyone knew when they exited the ballpark was this: One of these days, one of these weeks, one of these months, whenever the commissioner decided to lift the first suspended game in the history of postseason baseball, the Phillies, the Rays, and the rest of humanity were going to find Game 5 of this World Series, in theory, exactly where they left it.

Halfway through the sixth. Tie game, 2–2. The Phillies still leading the Series, three games to one. So they remained, again in theory, precisely where they were after Game 4—one win away from the second World Series championship in franchise history.

Yeah, it was all exactly the same, all right. Except nothing was the same.

A mere one day earlier, the Phillies had this Series set up in their ultimate dream scenario—one win away, with their most dominating starting pitcher lined up to pitch it.

Now, one soggy half-baked suspended-animation debacle later, they'd essentially wasted a Cole Hamels start.

And they were certain, at the time, that they were looking at having to deal with the terrifying prospect of facing David Price when play resumed.

And the two Rays hitters who were 0-for-the-Series—Carlos Pena and Evan Longoria—had finally remembered how to hit.

So you knew exactly what every Phillies fan in America was thinking as that rainwater was dripping all over their dreams: *Uh-oh.*

That would be the polite terminology for it, anyway.

In Philadelphia, nothing is ever easy. Nothing. So this mess just fit right in.

"Of course. We've gotta make the World Series memorable," laughed Hamels, after what was supposed to be the greatest night of his life had turned into Bud Selig's remake of *Singin' in the Rain.* "And this definitely will do so."

Hey, ya think?

Hamels tried his best to put a happy face on this insanity. But all you need to know about how his teammates felt about it was the sound of deafening silence all around him.

The manager, Charlie Manuel, wouldn't talk to the media afterward. And neither would many of the most prominent members of his team—Jimmy Rollins, Pat Burrell, Shane Victorino, and Jayson Werth, just to name a few.

You can draw your own conclusions as to why that was. But here are the conclusions we would draw if we were you:

- They were furious that this game wasn't stopped until Hamels had surrendered the tying run in the top of the sixth, even though the field had begun looking like a veritable Sea World attraction at least a half-hour earlier.
- They weren't happy that it was started in the first place, since glop had already begun falling out of the sky during batting practice and the worsening weather forecast was the No. 1 topic of pregame conversation—just ahead of how many layers of clothing they were all going to have to wear to avoid frostbite.
- And, most of all, they were incensed by the whole situation—having their best-laid World Series plans steamrolled by the needless rush to play a game in conditions more suitable for an Iditarod than the most important game of their careers.

"Hey, it sucks. Let's be honest," said closer Brad Lidge, one of the few Phillies who did address the media afterward. "But what choice do you have? We just have to come back here tomorrow and try to finish the job."

So how *were* these decisions made? Why did they start? Why did they keep on playing? Why did they stop play when they did?

Selig brought two umpires, Rays president Matt Silverman, and Phillies GM Pat Gillick to the postsuspension press conference afterward to try to explain it all—not to mention to try to make it as clear as possible that you couldn't hang this whole nightmare on him.

He talked about all the upbeat weather forecasts he'd been handed as late as 45 minutes before game time. He talked about the pregame

Mud and muck cover an on-deck batting circle after play was suspended during Game 5 of the World Series on October 27, 2008. The rain continued for so long in Philadelphia that the game was suspended for two days.

meeting he'd convened with the umpires, the grounds crew, the managers, the GMs—in short, everybody but Al Roker—in which they all decided, "Let's play."

And it was only in the fourth inning, Selig said, that he found himself "getting very nervous." Which caused him to make two different visits with the groundskeeper, in the fourth and fifth innings, to inquire about the state of the field.

Selig claimed he was told that it wasn't until the sixth inning that the field turned into a total river delta. And that's why the game was halted when it was.

But when players started describing the conditions afterward, suffice it to say they weren't quite as, uh, sunny about those elements as the commish.

Asked when *he* would have stopped this game, Rays reliever Trever Miller replied, "I would have said no later than the fourth inning. As soon as Jimmy Rollins had trouble with that fly ball [Rocco Baldelli's uncaught pop-up leading off the top of the fifth], right then and there that would have told everyone that conditions were not conducive to playing good baseball.

"That's what you want in the World Series," Miller said. "You want good baseball being played by the best players of the season. When Mother Nature is robbing you of that, it's time to put the tarp on and come back another day."

"Let me tell you," said his teammate, Carlos Pena. "That was bad. That was probably the worst conditions I've ever played under in my life. It was really, really cold. Windy. And it was raining nonstop. I mean, when do you ever see a puddle at home plate?"

Hamels said it was so hard to grip the ball, he never tried to throw a single curveball. And he could never get the right grip on his best pitch, his David Copperfield disappearing change-up. So he pumped about twice as many fastballs as he would on any other night. And this, remember, was supposed to be the most important night he'd ever spent on a pitcher's mound.

And then, when the fateful top of the sixth inning rolled around, the rain clearly changed the way the most pivotal inning of this game unfolded.

With two outs, nobody on, and an ocean pouring out of the heavens, B.J. Upton thunked a ground ball up the middle. It looked like a hit off the bat. But Rollins got there, got a glove on it, and then watched it wiggle out of his hands like a fish that had just slipped off his hook.

Within moments, Upton had stolen second—sliding right through a puddle the size of Delaware—and scored on Pena's two-out, two-strike single to left. And we had ourselves a tie game.

Before we get to the ramifications of that tie, though, let's go back to that fateful rally. Asked if he thought Rollins would have thrown Upton out had this been regular old weather—as opposed to monsoon season—Hamels had no doubt.

"On a normal day? Oh, yeah," he said. "Definitely. I think he might have caught Longoria's ball, too [i.e., the ground-ball single that drove in the Rays' first run, in the fourth]. But you know, that's the way luck [works] in baseball."

Yeah, and that luck worked for the commissioner, too. Because this game was now tied, he was able to walk into that press conference with his handy-dandy rule book and read off Rule 4.12.6—which allows for tie games that were already official to be suspended.

"I'll tell you what," said the Phillies' Matt Stairs. "To have a tie game, sixth inning, that makes Bud Selig and the boys pretty happy, because they didn't have to make a big decision, to let that game go through a 10-, 12-, 13-hour delay.... So the Big Man's happy. He didn't have to make that decision."

Ah, but what Matt Stairs didn't know—what, apparently, none of these players on either team knew—was that Selig had already made his big decision.

If the rules weren't going to permit him to suspend this game, he was going to have to go to Plan B. He was just going to have to impose martial law—or at least Selig's Law—and, essentially, suspend it anyway. By simply declaring the world's longest rain delay. Whether that took 24 hours, 48 hours, or all the way to Thanksgiving.

But whatever, Selig vowed, these teams were not going to finish this game "until we have decent weather conditions."

Gee, it's a shame he didn't have that same feeling before he allowed this game to start in the first place. But whatever, on this point, he made the right call. Players on both teams made it clear they would have been embarrassed to decide the World Series on a game that got rained out in the sixth inning.

"I truly think that would have been the worst World Series win in the face of baseball," Hamels said. "And I would not pride myself on being a world champion on a called game."

"The clinching game," said Miller, "should always be decided by nine innings and down to the last out. Not by Mother Nature or whatever else could be thrown at us. That's what the fans pay to see, and that's what we've worked our entire season to get to.

"For us not to get that hit right there…that would be awful. That would be the most miserable off-season I would have ever had, trying to swallow that one down. That stuff doesn't digest. Hopefully they recognize this, and in the winter meetings they establish some sort of protocol and this doesn't happen again."

Hey, good plan. Nothing like a little protocol, so that both teams at least would have gone into this situation knowing the rules they were playing under.

But now here's a better idea, an even better rule of thumb: We're pretty sure this won't be the last attack Mother Nature springs on a post-season baseball game. In fact, with the World Series scheduled to stretch into November in the future, the chances of a meteorological disaster way worse than this are almost a lock.

So how about if baseball makes a pact—right here, right now. The heck with the Fox primetime schedule. The heck with the old both-sides-have-to-play-in-it mind-set. How about this mind-set: If the weather forecast is scary enough before *any* postseason game to give the commissioner, in his own words, "significant trepidation" about playing, let's not start it. Okay?

It's that simple. What happened to the Phillies in Game 5 should never happen to any team in this situation. And Bud Selig knows it.

And here's what he also knows: It's a good thing the Phillies went on to win this World Series. Because if they hadn't, the always-magnanimous residents of Philadelphia weren't going to blame Charlie Manuel, the next three losing pitchers, or good old Mother Nature. They were going to blame him, Bud Selig.

And in the annals of Sports Figures Most Likely to Get Off the Hook in This Town, Bud should know this: There's a better chance that Philadelphians would forgive Joe Carter, T.O., and possibly even J.D. Drew than a commissioner whose inability to recognize a rain cloud cost these people a World Series parade.

Only in Philadelphia

PHILADELPHIA—In Philadelphia, folks are used to seeing the sky fall on their greatest sports parades.

Just usually, it's not quite this literally.

In Philadelphia, a place I confess I've lived most of my life, they know stuff happens in sports. They just wonder why it's mostly bad stuff. Especially when things seem way too good—by which we mean way too non-Philadelphian—to be true.

So Game 5 of the 2008 World Series fits right in. It's so utterly Philadelphian, they should place a DVD of it in William Penn's hand, way up there on top of City Hall.

One day, these folks were pouring through the gates of a ballpark they love, certain they were about to watch a team they love do something they'd witnessed once in their lives, their parents' lives, their grandparents' lives, the founding fathers' lives, and, when you get right down to it, even the dinosaurs' lives: Win a World Series.

Next thing they knew, there was more water falling on their heads than flowing between the banks of the Schuykill. Their sure-handed shortstop couldn't catch a pop-up. Their best pitcher couldn't grip the pitch that has made him what he is. And their happy little march to the parade floats had turned into an all-time weather debacle.

Only in Philadelphia.

Sooner or later—they hoped—Bud Selig was going to invite them all back to the ballpark to finish Game 5. And maybe, they hoped, it would all turn out fine for the Phillies and the millions of human beings whose mental health depended on them.

But that isn't what most of those humans were thinking 24 hours later, as those raindrops kept decending. Ohhhhh no. They were thinking even Mother Nature didn't want them to win. They were thinking it was their meteorological Bartman Moment. But above all, they were thinking this could only happen in Philadelphia, a place where heartbreak in sports is the specialty of the house.

Little did they suspect that the one thing they should have been remembering was that the team they'd surgically attached their psyches to wasn't thinking the way they were all thinking.

Asked, on the day after that deluge, if he was worried about his players' ability to put this weird turn of events behind them, Phillies manager Charlie Manuel replied, "I don't think there's going to be any problem at all. I think we've been resilient now for the last couple of years. I think we know exactly where we're going and what we want to do. We're going to be ready."

Asked the night before what he would tell the fans who had shown up for Game 5 at Citizens Bank Park believing they were about to see their team win the World Series, Phillies ace Cole Hamels retorted, "That's what we're believing. And that's what we still believe. Now it won't obviously be tonight. But tomorrow. That's what we really want to do. We want to do it in Philly, in front of the fans who have really been there for us all year."

Of course, every team says stuff like that about its fans this time of year. But this time, it was different. This time, it was those fans—those weary, desperate, beaten-down, angst-ridden, broken dreamers—who had become one of the most intriguing parts of this plotline.

These people had spent the last parade-free quarter-century walking around with such a profound, universal sense of dread that every one of them should have had their own personal psychological counselor assigned to them.

They weren't merely aware of all the natural sporting disasters that had befallen their teams through the years—from Chico Ruiz to the Fog Bowl, from Black Friday to Smarty Jones. They'd spent much of their lives contemplating just how and when their next nightmare was about to demolish their spirit, with one swing of the big old sporting wrecking ball.

But then something amazing happened. There was something about this team that gave them faith and the courage to conquer that dread.

They'd just seen their team win one game on a 2:00 AM dribbler down the line and another on a mighty home run by a pitcher they'd never before confused with Mike Schmidt. They found their team leading this World Series three games to one. And all of a sudden, for once in their lives, they were convinced this was their time, that it was finally safe to trust this team.

That's a phenomenon, you understand, that's more rare in this universe than the Aurora Borealis. So when it erupted, it was so striking that even these players themselves noticed it.

"Even when we'd lose a game late in the season," said third baseman Greg Dobbs, "the stuff we'd hear was, 'That's okay, boys. Get 'em tomorrow.' Not, 'Boo, you suck.' We got none of that. So you know how people say you learn more about yourselves and others when you face adversity? I think that's something I learned from the fans. I realized that these fans have actually turned the corner."

But in Philadelphia, it's never a shock that, just when they least expect it, the corner is always waiting to turn on them. So of course it turned. One more time.

And, naturally, it wasn't even the first time the weather gods did the turning. It was 31 years since another October monsoon washed away another Phillies team's dreams—31 years since the Phillies and Dodgers played an entire LCS-ending game in conditions right out of the set of *The Perfect Storm*. And, *of course*, people in Philadelphia spent every waking waterlogged hour reminiscing about that day—because no good Philadelphia sports horror story deserves to be put out of its misery. Ever.

But at least, unlike that day, the commissioner of baseball didn't pretend that this time around it wasn't even raining. At least this time, the commish noticed those raindrops and placed this game in a state of suspended animation.

So at least this time—with three and a half innings left to be played in Game 5—there was still a chance for this Phillies team to rewrite this story.

Or not.

So that was the plotline hovering over this World Series as the planet waited for Game 5 to resume.

If, somehow, the Phillies hadn't gone on to win, this World Series would have left a scar on their fan base the size of the King of Prussia Mall.

But because they did, it turned this goofy weather mess into something to laugh about during every October deluge for the next thousand years.

So Part 2 of this game would be more than a mere sporting event, friends. It would be a life-altering event for an entire community. Would these people get their parade and release their demons? Or would one horrendously ill-timed act of nature drive them deeper into the Cuckoo's Nest?

It was all about to be played out on a soggy October baseball field. Only in Philadelphia.

Worth the Wait

PHILADELPHIA—For a quarter of a century, they'd waited for this night, waited for this moment.

For a quarter of a century, they'd watched these scenes happen in somebody else's town, on somebody else's field of dreams.

Seasons came. Seasons went. Baseball seasons. Football seasons. Basketball seasons. Hockey seasons. They never ended this way—not one stinking one of them. Not in Philadelphia—the city where these sorts of dreams never came true.

And then, on a wintry night in October, in the cliffhanger episode of *A Funny Thing Happened on the Way to the Parade Floats*, it happened.

It was 9:58 PM in the Eastern Time Zone. The perfect closer, Brad Lidge, finished off the perfect season with the perfect pitch.

The hitter standing 60 feet away, Tampa Bay's Eric Hinske, swung through one last invisible slider. And as Brad Lidge collapsed to his knees and euphoria erupted all around him, you could almost feel the sky clearing and the universe shifting.

The Phillies had won the World Series, won it in five astounding games, won it by finishing off a 4–3 win over Tampa Bay they'd had to wait 46 waterlogged hours just to complete.

But that's not all. For the city they play in, the wait was over. A wait that had consumed every man, woman, and child; every Mummer; every pretzel baker; every cheesesteak chomper; every boobird.

A wait that had dragged them all through 25 years and 98 combined seasons of misery and heartbreak, seasons whose only common trait was that they'd all managed to last just a little too long.

It was the longest wait, by far, of the 13 metropolitan areas in America with teams in all four major sports. No other metropolis out there—anywhere—was within eight years.

And then, with one pitch, with one euphoric shriek in the night—in 45,000-part harmony—it was over. And life in Philadelphia may never be the same.

"For all these years," said Jimmy Rollins as fireworks crackled through the night, "the part of playing here that upset me the most was that I was always home in October, watching somebody else celebrate.

"But not this year," said the man who first opened his mouth and dared them all to reach for this chunk of the sky. "This year, *we* get to celebrate."

If you live in Kansas or New Mexico or Maine, you may not fully understand the meaning of all this. So we'll try to spell it out for you.

How long did Philadelphians have to wait? In between championships, their four pro teams played a combined 9,029 games without ever producing a night quite like this.

There were titles in Green Bay and Edmonton and East Rutherford, New Jersey. There were parades in Charlotte and Calgary and San Antonio. But never in Philly. Not once.

Philadelphia's four teams reached the postseason 47 times in all those years—and got bounced out of the postseason in all 47 of them. Seven of those teams made it all the way to the final round of that postseason. All seven watched somebody else spraying the champagne.

But of all those franchises, none dragged its fans through the funny farm more than the Phillies.

From 1984 through 2006, they reached the postseason just once in 23 seasons. They lost more games in that time than any team in their league except the Pirates.

They watched the Royals win a World Series. They watched the Diamondbacks win a World Series. They watched the Marlins win two of them. The Red Sox finally won. The White Sox finally won. But the Phillies just kept wallowing in that muck, looking for the formula that would lead them to a night like this.

So what were the odds that, in the 4,416th game they'd played since the last title in their town, it was the local baseball team that finally parted the polluted waters?

"When I was a kid, back in 1980, baseball was still exciting here," said Jamie Moyer, the only Phillie who could say he actually attended the parade of the 1980 World Series champs. "Back then, people lived for the game around here. So it's funny. Last year, one of our beat writers said to me, 'Do you realize you guys, as a team, brought baseball back to Philadelphia?'

"I never really looked at it that way. I never really thought about it that way, that we had brought baseball back to Philadelphia. He said, 'It's something that had been lost here for a lot of years.' And I said, 'You know what? If that's the case, that's really cool. That in our own small way, we've been able to bring baseball back to Philadelphia, to bring the Phillies back on the map.'"

And now, of course, they're the team that actually owns that map.

What a concept.

Before this night, they'd won one World Series in the first 125 years in their history. They'd lost more games than any team in any professional sport in North America. They were a team that hadn't just dropped off their own city's map. There was a time they'd practically toppled off their own sport's map. But not anymore.

As late as mid-September, these Phillies were a team dangling from the National League cliff—three and a half games behind the Mets in the NL East, four games back of the Brewers in the wild-card free-for-all. No one could have seen then that a parade was in their future.

But all they did after that was go 24–6. Yeah, 24–6. Only four World Series winners in history—just two of them in the last 94 years—ever had a better finish than that.

"You always see that every year, don't you?" said outfielder Geoff Jenkins. "There's always that one team that gets hot at the right time."

Yeah, you always see it, all right. You just never saw it in this town, from this team. Until now.

These Phillies were so hot, they won games in this World Series they had no business winning. A game in which they went 0-for-13 with men in scoring position. A game that lasted till 1:47 AM. A game in which Joltin' Joe Blanton was their home-run hero.

But they saved their grand finale for the goofiest game of all. A game with a 46-hour rain delay. A game divided into a two-part soap opera. A game so strange that even though it ended on a Wednesday night, history will always tell us it was played on a Monday night, thanks to that tricky suspension passage in Bud Selig's rulebook.

It was all so bizarre, all so unprecedented, it was hard to know what these teams would encounter when the glop finally stopped falling out of the sky and it was safe to come back to the ballpark.

One of the big questions in the minds of Phillies players, Moyer said, was whether the seats would even be full. Who knows how many of the 45,000 people sitting in those seats after the Game 5 rain delay had left town, had other stuff on their plate, or had even lost their ticket stubs, he wondered.

Three Strikes—Philly File Edition

Jamie Moyer said during the World Series that the longer you wait for things, the more you appreciate them. If that's the case, there might not be any city in America that could have appreciated watching those parade floats more than Philadelphia.

How long had they all waited? How long is 25 years in Philly-sports-fan years? Here's how long:

STRIKE ONE—THOSE PHUTILE PHILLIES DEPT.: Nobody was responsible for more Philadelphia futility during that 25-year title drought than the Phillies. In between championships—their own and their city's—you could measure the Phillies' slice of eternity this way:

- They played 4,127 games in between Philadelphia champagne showers—37 postseason games and 4,090 regular-season games—and lost 2,111 of them.
- They played 4,452 games, including the postseason, in between their 1980 World Series parade and Game 5 in 2008—and lost 2,252 of them.
- All these teams played in more postseason series than the Phillies between World Series parades: The Indians, A's, Astros, Mets, and Angels. And in the 25 years between Philadelphia championships, the Twins, Giants, Padres, and White Sox all played in at least as many postseason series as the Phillies.
- 206 pitchers won at least one game for the Phillies in between those parades, including all these mystery guests: Eddie Oropesa, Ed Vosberg, Fernando Valenzuela, Alex Madrid, Yorkis Perez, Calvin Maduro, and Starvin' Marvin Freeman.
- And 376 players got at least one hit for the Phillies in between titles, including (of course): Larry Andersen, Billy Almon, A.J. Hinch, T.J. Bohn, P.J. Forbes, J.R. Phillips, Jeff Manto, and a man who got a hit at 4:41 AM—Mitch Williams.

STRIKE TWO—SUPPORTING CAST DEPT.: But the Phillies, obviously, weren't the only team that did its part to keep that parade drought going. Here's how Philadelphia's other three teams contributed:

- The Eagles played 390 regular-season games between Philly parades, made the playoffs 12 times, and played 20 playoff games—but made it to only one Super Bowl and (yep) lost it. So that comes to 410 games.
- The Flyers played 1,568 regular-season games, made the playoffs 18 times, played 212 playoff games, and made it to the Stanley Cup finals three times—but (as you may have heard someplace) went 0-for-3. That adds up to 1,780 games.
- And the Sixers played 1,926 regular-season games, made the playoffs 14 times, played 125 playoff games, and made it to the NBA finals once. So that's 2,051 games between titles—including one in the middle of Game 5 of the World Series.
- So that's 4,141 games those three teams played—and not one of them ended in the kind of scene that unfolded October 28, 2008, night at Citizens Bank Park.

STRIKE THREE—EVERYWHERE BUT HERE DEPT.: So how many celebrations did people in Philadelphia have to witness in every town but their own through the years? Way more than they'd all like to count up. So I did it for them:

- Seventeen different teams won at least one World Series in the years that the Phillies were winning none. That group includes the Royals, Orioles, Twins, Reds, Blue Jays, Marlins, Diamondbacks, White Sox, Angels, and those accursed Red Sox.
- All these towns got to celebrate a title in one of those other sports in the years that Philadelphia was celebrating zero titles: Green Bay, Edmonton, Indianapolis, Calgary, Charlotte, San Antonio, and East Rutherford.
- And just to make this drought especially fun for all those poor Philadelphians, they had to watch New York–based teams win 16 titles (including events in the scenic Meadowlands), New England teams win eight titles, and Chicago teams win eight titles—all during the time that their teams were winning no titles.

But now their drought is over. Will the miracles never cease?

"I was looking around during [batting practice], and I was thinking, *Boy, there's not a whole lot of people here,*" Moyer said. "But by the start of this game, this place was full."

And not just full, said Chase Utley, "This place was rocking."

And then up marched Jenkins toward home plate to kick off the long-awaited bottom of the sixth. He'd been told a mere 10 minutes earlier by manager Charlie Manuel that he'd be the guy leading off, pinch-hitting for pitcher Cole Hamels, whose last pitch was thrown two days earlier. But Geoff Jenkins, a missing person throughout this whole wild month, couldn't possibly have been more grateful for that one last chance.

Jenkins hadn't gotten a hit in over a month, since a September 28 single against the Nationals. But he laser-beamed a double into the right-center-field gap. And the house was shaking.

"When Jenks hit that double," laughed Rollins, "the decibel level was off the charts."

One pitch later, Rollins bunted him to third. Six pitches after that, Jayson Werth blooped a single a millimeter beyond the glove of Akinori Iwamura. And Jenkins found himself crossing home plate for the first time since August 11—79 days ago.

"Biggest moment of my whole career," he said.

That lead didn't last long, thanks to a seventh-inning Rocco Baldelli bomb that turned into the first home run allowed by reliever Ryan Madson in Philadelphia in exactly six months. But moments later, Utley made the kind of play that has made him a star—backhanding an Iwamura chopper up the middle, faking a throw to first and then nailing Jason Barlett, the go-ahead run, at the plate. And the Phillies never looked back.

Next thing they knew, Pat Burrell led off the bottom of the seventh with a double off the top of the left-center-field fence—his only hit of this World Series and his final hit as a Phillie. A half-dozen pitches later,

Pedro Feliz gave the Phillies back the lead with a rope through the drawn-in infield. And from Bryn Mawr to Bensalem, there wasn't anyone breathing who couldn't smell a parade.

It was 9:46 when Lidge burst through the bullpen gates and began trotting toward the mound. Flashbulbs popped. Rally towels gyrated. The sound rumbling out of this ballpark had to be audible in West Virginia.

The Phillies were 93–0 when leading after eight. Lidge was 47-for-47 when a save was on the line. This was their kind of script.

And then there he was, only a few minutes later, one strike away. Hinske rocked in the batter's box. The tying run was on second. The house was rattling. And Brad Lidge had to take a quick stroll behind the mound, just to remember how to breathe.

"With two strikes, I had to step off the mound, because, honestly, I don't even know what was going through my mind," he said. "I was going to throw my best pitch the way I know how to. But I mean, you can't feel yourself. I honestly couldn't feel myself. It felt like the first time I ever pitched in a big-league game. Your legs are heavy, and you have to take a big, deep breath just to be able to pitch."

But finally, he turned, headed back up to the rubber, and launched one final untouchable slider. What followed was a slice of heaven that every pitcher who ever lived has dreamed about: The strikeout that wins your team the World Series.

Lidge crumbled to both knees. His catcher, Carlos Ruiz, raced into his arms. Then that tender scene was interrupted by the sight of a 6'4", 256-pound behemoth doing a full-gainer, diving on top of both of them.

Asked if he was trying to kill his pitcher and catcher, Ryan Howard chuckled, "Oh, most definitely. But then, when the rest of the pile came along, I knew that was a bad idea."

Carlos Ruiz celebrates with relief pitcher Brad Lidge after the final out in Game 5 of the World Series to give the Phillies the championship on October 29, 2008.

The rest of it, though—was the *whole* idea. Fireworks sparkling...four coaches hugging Charlie Manuel at once...Jimmy Rollins pointing toward the sky.

Howard picking himself up and racing around the field, waving the championship flag, accompanied by a swarm of teammates, photographers, and police officers...a fan holding up a sign that read "Good night, Joe Carter"...and an entire city roaring, rumbling, laughing, crying, all at once.

"I think when you high-five the cops, and you're hugging the grounds crew, and you just see the jubilation in everybody out there, it really kind of hits you that wow, you just won the whole damn thing," said Geoff Jenkins, trying to digest it all. "And you just can't describe what that means to everybody.... They feel they won a title just like we did."

But they feel that way, of course, because, on a powerful human level, they did. They might not have played a single game—not in 2008, not for that whole painful, title-free quarter-century. But they did something just as powerful.

"They lived it," said Jamie Moyer.

Moyer stood there at his locker with the ultimate souvenir—the pitcher's rubber—at his feet. And, as the senior member of this team, a born-and-raised Philadelphian, a guy who had waited 23 seasons for this moment to happen to him, he got it more than anyone else around him.

It makes no sense, logically, that what happens on a baseball field— any baseball field—could change other people's lives in any meaningful way. But throughout this exhilarating October, Jamie Moyer had made a point of stopping every night to look around and take in every unforgettable moment. So he knew exactly how profoundly this had changed people's lives.

The Philadelphia Phillies celebrate after winning the rain-delayed Game 5 of the World Series in Philadelphia on October 29, 2008. The Phillies defeated the Tampa Bay Rays 4–3 to win the series.

"And I think that's great," he said. "That's what baseball does. There are going to be people today, tomorrow, next week, next month, next year saying, 'I was blank-blank-blank when the Phillies won the World Series.' And that's pretty cool, to have a story of wherever they were when the Phillies won the World Series: 'I was in the parking lot. I was in the stands. I was at a bar. I was having dinner. I was coming back from a trip and I couldn't see it, so I listened to it in the car.' And to me, that's kind of cool, because that's what baseball does for people. I just think that's why it's so special."

What made it special was that he and these men he plays with had just blown away the biggest cloud in America. And the best part of it all was, that cloud is never coming back. And they sensed it—all of them.

"When you win, it's forever," said Geoff Jenkins. "It's forever, man. And that's a great feeling."

World Series, Game 5,
October 27 and 29, 2008, at Philadelphia
Phillies 4, Rays 3

Tampa Bay	AB	R	H	RBI	BB	SO	LOB	AVG
Iwamura, 2B	4	0	2	0	0	1	0	.263
Crawford, LF	4	0	1	0	0	0	1	.263
Upton, CF	4	1	1	0	0	0	1	.250
Pena, 1B	4	1	2	1	0	0	0	.118
Price, P	0	0	0	0	0	0	0	.000
Longoria, 3B	4	0	1	1	0	0	1	.050
Navarro, C	3	0	1	0	1	1	1	.353
1-Perez, F, PR	0	0	0	0	0	0	0	.000
Baldelli, RF	3	1	1	1	0	0	1	.167
a-Zobrist, PH	1	0	0	0	0	0	1	.143
Bartlett, SS	3	0	1	0	0	0	1	.214
b-Hinske, PH	1	0	0	0	0	1	1	.500
Kazmir, P	2	0	0	0	0	2	0	.000
Balfour, P	0	0	0	0	0	0	0	.000
Howell, P	0	0	0	0	0	0	0	.000
Bradford, P	0	0	0	0	0	0	0	.000
Aybar, 1B	0	0	0	0	0	0	0	.250
Totals	33	3	10	3	1	5	8	

Philadelphia	AB	R	H	RBI	BB	SO	LOB	AVG
Rollins, SS	3	0	0	0	1	0	0	.227
Werth, RF	3	1	2	1	2	1	0	.444
Utley, 2B	3	1	0	0	1	1	0	.167
Howard, 1B	4	0	0	0	1	3	4	.286
Burrell, LF	2	0	1	0	2	0	0	.071
1-Bruntlett,								
PR-LF	0	1	0	0	0	0	0	.333
Victorino, CF	4	0	1	2	0	1	3	.250
Feliz, 3B	4	0	2	1	0	1	2	.333
Ruiz, C	4	0	1	0	0	0	6	.375
Hamels, P	2	0	0	0	0	1	1	.000
a-Jenkins, PH	1	1	1	0	0	0	0	.500
Madson, P	0	0	0	0	0	0	0	.000
Romero, P	1	0	0	0	0	0	1	.000
Lidge, P	0	0	0	0	0	0	0	.000
Totals	31	4	8	4	7	8	22	

a-Lined out for Baldelli in the 9th. b-Struck out for Bartlett in the 9th.
1-Ran for Navarro in the 9th.

BATTING
2B: Pena (1, Hamels).
HR: Baldelli (1, 7th inning off Madson, 0 on, 1 out).
TB: Iwamura 2; Crawford; Upton; Pena 3; Longoria; Navarro; Baldelli 4; Bartlett.
RBI: Longoria (2), Pena (2), Baldelli (1).
2-out RBI: Pena.
Runners left in scoring position, 2 out: Longoria; Hinske.
S: Howell.
GIDP: Navarro; Bartlett; Upton.
Team LOB: 5.

BASERUNNING
SB: Perez, F (1, 2nd base off Lidge/Ruiz), Upton (4, 2nd base off Hamels/Ruiz).

a-Doubled for Hamels in the 6th.
1-Ran for Burrell in the 7th.

BATTING
2B: Jenkins (1, Balfour), Burrell (1, Howell).
TB: Werth 2; Burrell 2; Victorino; Feliz 2; Ruiz; Jenkins 2.
RBI: Victorino 2 (2), Werth (3), Feliz (2).
2-out RBI: Victorino 2.
Runners left in scoring position, 2 out: Ruiz 3; Utley 2; Howard 2.
S: Rollins.
Team LOB: 12.

BASERUNNING
SB: Werth (3, 2nd base off Howell/Navarro), Utley (3, 2nd base off Price/Navarro).

FIELDING
E: Rollins (1, fielding).
PB: Ruiz (1).
DP: 3 (Rollins-Utley-Howard 2, Utley-Howard).

Tampa Bay	IP	H	R	ER	BB	SO	HR	ERA
Kazmir	4.0	4	2	2	6	5	0	4.50
Balfour	1.1	2	1	1	0	0	0	3.00
Howell (L, 0-2)	0.2	1	1	1	0	1	0	7.71
Bradford	1.0	1	0	0	0	0	0	0.00
Price	1.0	0	0	0	1	2	0	2.70

Philadelphia	IP	H	R	ER	BB	SO	HR	ERA
Hamels	6.0	5	2	2	1	3	0	2.77
Madson (BS, 2)	0.2	2	1	1	0	1	1	4.91
Romero (W, 2-0)	1.1	2	0	0	0	0	0	0.00
Lidge (S, 2)	1.0	1	0	0	0	1	0	0.00

Kazmir pitched to 2 batters in the 5th; Howell pitched to 1 batter in the 7th.

HBP: Utley (by Kazmir); Pitches-strikes: Kazmir 103-62, Balfour 21-16, Howell 7-6, Bradford 10-9, Price 20-9, Hamels 75-48, Madson 9-8, Romero 14-8, Lidge 16-13; Groundouts-flyouts: Kazmir 2-5, Balfour 1-3, Howell 0-1, Bradford 3-0, Price 0-1, Hamels 11-4, Madson 1-0, Romero 2-1, Lidge 0-2; Batters faced: Kazmir 23, Balfour 6, Howell 3, Bradford 4, Price 4, Hamels 23, Madson 4, Romero 4, Lidge 4; Inherited runners-scored: Balfour 2-0, Howell 1-0, Bradford 1-1, Romero 1-0; Umpires: HP: Jeff Kellogg. 1B: Tim Tschida. 2B: Tim Welke. 3B: Kerwin Danley. LF: Fieldin Culbreth. RF: Tom Hallion.

Weather: 47 degrees, drizzle; Wind: 16 mph, L to R; T: 3:28 (:30 delay); Att: 45,940.

Useless
Information

- The Phillies were the first team to have a potential clinching game in the World Series delayed by rain since the Mets and Red Sox had to wait an extra day before playing Game 7 of the 1986 World Series, thanks to A) Bill Buckner (and accomplices) and B) a rainout the night after the Buckner Game.

- The last time the weather forced a team to wait multiple days to play a potential World Series clincher was 1975, when Game 6 in Boston was rained out for three straight days with the Reds leading three games to one.

- What's the all-time record for longest wait to play (or finish) one World Series game? How about six days. That's how long the A's and Giants waited to play Game 4 of the 1911 Series—in Philadelphia.

- Could Cole Hamels possibly have been more efficient in this postseason? In his 35 October innings, he hung a zero in 28 of them. And in all seven of the innings in which he was scored on, he gave up just one run.

- Only the rain kept all five Phillies starters from working into the seventh inning in this World Series. The Rays starters, on the other hand, pitched a combined 25⅔ innings in five games—and allowed 53 base runners (counting those who reached on errors). Yikes.

Useless Information

- From September 11 to the World Series victory podium, the Phillies finished 2008 by going 24–6 in their last 30 games. Only four World Series winners ever had a better final 30 games than that, according to the Elias Sports Bureau—the 1970 Orioles (26–4), 1942 Cardinals (25–5), 1914 Braves (25–5), and 1908 Cubs (25–5).

- The Phillies played seven games in Philadelphia during the 2008 postseason—and won every darned one of them. Only one other team ever went 7–0 at home during a single postseason—the 1999 Yankees.

- Just three teams in history ever went more years between World Series victories than the 28 years the Phillies waited—the White Sox (88 years, from 1917–2005), the Red Sox (86 years, from 1918–2004), and the Pirates (35 years, from 1925–1960). Of course, that list could change dramatically if the Cubs, Indians, Giants, or Pirates ever win again one of these centuries.

- Here's official proof that the Phillies did it with mirrors: Their two World Series titles came in '80 and '08. And the closer who got the last out in those World Series wore No. 45 (Tug McGraw) and No. 54 (Brad Lidge).

- Finally, now that the Phillies are off the schneid, which four-sport city has gone the longest without any of its pro teams winning a championship? That would be the great metropolis of Minneapolis. Their last title was in 1991, courtesy of Jack Morris and the Twins.